W Crew Stroke to Bow

A Dad's Waterscape View of Women's Intercollegiate Rowing

Richard J. Seif
Ellen K. Zilly

First Edition
Activities Press, Inc.
Mentor, Ohio

THE COVER
The last 200 meters of the 2002 Big Ten Championship
First Varsity Eight race hosted by Michigan State University.
The event marked the 3rd annual Big Ten Championship
with seven Big Ten teams participating at Lake Ovid, near
East Lansing, Michigan. The teams in the picture (front to back) are:
The Ohio State University, University of Michigan, and Michigan
State University. The Ohio State University won the race
and won the Championship in 2002.

W Crew
Stroke to Bow

Richard J. Seif
Ellen K. Zilly

Published by:
Activities Press
7181 Industrial Park Blvd.
Mentor OH 44060 U.S.A.
www.activitiespress.com

All rights of the book are reserved. Absolutely no part of the book may be reproduced or transmitted in any form or by any means: electronic, or mechanical, including photocopying, recording, or by any information storage and retrieval system without expressed written permission from the authors, except for the inclusion of brief quotations in a review.

Copyright ©2004, by Richard J Seif

Printed in the United States of America

Publisher's Cataloging-in-Publication
(Provided by Quality Books, Inc.)

Seif, Richard J.
    W crew stroke to bow : a dad's waterscape view of women's intercollegiate rowing / Richard J. Seif with Ellen K. Zilly. - 1st ed.
    p. cm.
    Includes bibliographical references and index.

    1. Rowing-United States. 2. Women rowers-United States. 3. Sports for women-United States. 4. College sports-United States. I. Zilly, Ellen K. II. Title

GV796.S45 2004   797.1'23
                                  QBI04-200108

DISCLAIMER

This book is designed to inform and inspire the reader about the sport of college rowing for women. It is sold with the understanding that the publisher and authors are not engaged in rendering consulting services on the subject.

It is not the purpose of this book to reprint all the information that is otherwise available to authors and other creative people, but to complement, amplify, and supplement other writings. For more information, see the many references in the Appendix, marked "Sources."

Every effort has been made to make this book as complete and accurate as possible. However, there may be mistakes, either typographical or in content. Therefore, this text should be used only as general information and not as the ultimate authority on the subject.

Also, this book contains information on writing and publishing only up to the printing date.

The purpose of the book is to educate and inspire. The authors and Activities Press Publishing shall not have the liability or responsibility to any person or entity with respect to any loss or damage caused directly or indirectly by the information contained in this book.

TABLE OF CONTENTS

Acknowledgements i
Foreword iii
A Word from the Author v
Chapter 1   Wanted: Female Athletes 5'10" and Taller 1
Chapter 2   Women's Crew Surfaces 7
Chapter 3   Know Your Row 15
Chapter 4   Every Seat Counts 25
Chapter 5   Big Commitment Inside .41
Chapter 6   Spring Forward 53
Chapter 7   It's A Shell Game 61
Chapter 8   Every Race Has Its Course 71
Chapter 9   All In Your Head 81
Chapter 10   Sprint to the Finish 87
Chapter 11   Battle of the Parents 105
Chapter 12   Crew Coverage 113
Chapter 13   "Rowed" to the Sweep 16 119
Chapter 14   Big Ten Breaks the Ice .129
Chapter 15   Beyond Rowing 137
Appendix
    Sources 147
    Women's Collegiate Rowing Programs-2004 Head Coaches .149
Index 153
About the Authors 155
Quick Order Form 157

ACKNOWLEDGEMENTS

Thanks to the women: my wife, Carol, for her moral support; my two rowing daughters, Kirsten and Lindsay, for their input and honest review; Krista Buzzell, All-American stroke, for her inner thoughts about rowing and life; Mary Fening, for her creative talent; Ellen Zilly, for her writing skills, illustrations and crew insights; Bebe Bryans, M.S.U. Head Coach for women's crew from 1997-2004*, for her coaching perspective.

Thanks to the men: my son, Derrek, for his overview; Matt Weise, M.S.U. Assistant Coach for women's crew from 1997-2004*, for his technical input; Glenn Detrick, Rob Falls, and Patrick Morin for their professional critique.

Richard J. Seif

* In June 2004, Bebe Bryans became head coach for women's crew at the University of Wisconsin, and Matt Weise was named head coach for women's crew at Michigan State University.

FOREWORD

Women's crew is one of the most demanding sports for female athletes in all of intercollegiate competition. The women who row require a combination of technique, strength, stamina, and heart in order to succeed. Because rowing is more of a participant sport than a spectator sport, the talent and dedication required of these athletes often go unnoticed.

Mr. Seif and Ms. Zilly have captured the very essence of what women's collegiate crew is all about. I believe their total waterscape view will heighten awareness, understanding, and appreciation for all who are connected to this great sport. Read this book and you will have the knowledge of a coach, the passion of a rower, and a total grasp of what it takes for a women's crew team to become NCAA Championship caliber.

Bebe Bryans
Head Coach, Women's Crew
  Georgetown University (1992-1997)
  Michigan State University (1997-2004)
  University of Wisconsin (2004-present)

A WORD FROM THE AUTHOR

In the Name of the Father and Daughter

There is only one famous crew Dad: Henry Emerson "Dad" Vail, an early 20th century professional sculler and University of Wisconsin rowing coach. Today's largest collegiate U.S.A. regatta is held on Philadelphia's Schuylkill River and is known as the Dad Vail Rowing Championship.

Although I am no "Dad" Vail, I am a Dad who likes nothing better than watching his own kids succeed at sports. Since the days of T-ball and "herd ball," soccer for little kids, I have enjoyed both coaching and watching my three children as they succeeded in sports. Sports teach winning and losing in life. Having raised a son and two daughters in the state of Ohio, I was most familiar with football, basketball, baseball, softball, and volleyball. After 22 years, my most involved hobby of "kid sport" watching came to a sudden close when my youngest daughter "rowed out" of her four years of eligibility at Michigan State University. Now, going through withdrawal from this intense hobby, I decided to spend time sharing some insights into one of the best sports created for young women, Intercollegiate Crew.

My oldest daughter, Lindsay, was the family catalyst to women's crew. As a collegiate freshman, and burned out from high school volleyball, she joined the Club Crew Team at Penn State University. Lindsay's crew activity inspired her younger sister, Kirsten, to "walk on" the crew team at

Michigan State University. It was her four years of varsity rowing that led to a captivating experience for me and my wife. With those crew years finally finished, I began my rowing withdrawal as a Novice Crew Dad.

With weekend time on my hands, I decided to share some insights of a father's participation in four years with the Michigan State Women's Crew team. With scattered information and few books written on the subject, I thought that I might help other parents and rowers learn about this sport, which was recently modernized by the NCAA, and especially the Big Ten, courtesy of Title IX. As a father watching my daughter compete, I learned more and more about the intricacies of the sport as I went through her four varsity years. With each passing year, I not only gained more passion for the sport and all its surroundings, but also became fairly knowledgeable about it. I knew that I graduated from "Novice Crew Dad" status when I had to explain to a veteran Brown University parent what it meant when their team did not qualify for the grand finals at the NCAA Championships. This parent from Brown's women's crew experienced nothing but successes and never had to know the facts about the Petite Finals. I decided then that I wanted to share how this sport is set up so the Midwest "dummies" like me could learn, and the whole crew community could have information in one book about this great women's collegiate opportunity.

My youngest daughter, Kirsten, was an athlete, but had never rowed in her life when she first attended Michigan State in 1999. Being 6' tall and a "walk on," she had the wonderful experience of being coached at first by Assistant Coach Matt Weise, a former M.S.U. Club rower and coach. As Kirsten moved up to the varsity 8+, she had the great coaching experience from head M.S.U. Coach, Bebe Bryans. Bebe, an NCAA Championship swimmer and a master's world championship rower, endorses the best athlete philosophy. Given the raw talent, her mission is to teach rowing techniques to a good athlete and bring her to the level of NCAA Final's caliber. I watched how she did this with

A WORD FROM THE AUTHOR:
IN THE NAME OF THE FATHER AND DAUGHTER

Kirsten and her teammates, as well as how she created a competitive philosophy in a sport like it was meant to be. Her coaching vision was one key inspiration for me to write this book. Hopefully, this writing will spread greater information and enthusiasm for the sport. Even parents on the east and west coasts of the U.S.A. who grew up with rowing, may find new information as well as a consolidated reference of their beloved sport. With increased parental knowledge, Bebe and other coaches will be able to focus their coaching efforts on building the talents of young women and not spend time explaining the sport to the Novice Crew Dads like me-at least the Midwest Dads.

0.1 M.S.U. Coaches
Matt Weise and Bebe Bryans (1997-2004)

I have teamed up with Ellen Zilly, a four-year varsity rower for The Ohio State University. With her experience in Division I, including the NCAA Championships, Ellen has captured the physical and mental insights from a female rower's perspective of this highly demanding sport.

It is my intent for you to read this book, gain an inside look into a new found women's athletic passion, and understand not only what this growing college sport is all about, but what it represents: Preparation for life's journey.

By writing this book, I have satisfied my Crew Dad withdrawal pains, and will hopefully help educate and inspire you about Women's Crew.

I wrote the book for every father who has a daughter.

I wrote the book for every father whose daughter competes in sports.

I wrote the book for every father whose daughter competes in an NCAA varsity sport.

I wrote this book for every father whose daughter rows her ass off in Crew.

I wrote this book for every daughter who leaves everything she has on the water.

I wrote this book in the "name of the father and daughter."

0.2 Novice Crew Dad at Windermere Classic
Redwood Shores, California - 2003

CHAPTER 1

Wanted:
Female Athletes 5'10" and Taller

I was standing at the finish line at Lake Ovid, near East Lansing, Michigan. My heart was in my throat as three shells were coming directly at me, and knowing at the same time my daughter's heart rate was at its max and her lungs were gasping for oxygen. All twenty-four women were pulling as hard as they could while they fought off the lactic acid burn in their legs and arms.

Each coxswain (cox) was frantically yelling out the stroke set as this was the last 200 meters of the Big Ten Championship and Ohio State, Michigan, and Michigan State were all within a deck length (three feet) to win the first varsity eight event. With my binoculars around my neck and my camera held to my cheekbone, I watched through the telephoto lens as they neared the finish line. All the teams, coaches, and parents were screaming their guts out on the bank of the lake. The rowers were oblivious to the noise and were in a "zone," eyes fixed, afraid to even peek at their competition for fear of rocking the boat and losing precious tenths of a second. My daughter was in seat 4, the shell's engine, and stroking with authority, eyes straight ahead, focusing on every movement of the stern four to make sure the seam of the boat did not rip.

As the teams crossed the finish line and the horn sounded in close sequence, there were only 2.5 seconds difference between the three shells. Ohio State finished first with a time of 6:29.5, Michigan placed second at 6:31.2 and Michigan State was third at 6:32.0. The date was May 4, 2002, and marked the completion of the third Big Ten Championship for women's crew with the most exciting and exhilarating competition in its young Big Ten history.

1.1   2002 Big Ten Championships - Lake Ovid

U.S.A. Development

Women's ("W") crew has rapidly developed in the Big Ten Conference. Traditionally, this sport was featured on the East and West Coasts, but now seven out of eleven schools in the conference have "W" crew as a sanctioned varsity sport. In addition to Ohio State, Michigan and Michigan State, Wisconsin has always had a rowing tradition for both men and women competing at a very high level.

Recently, the universities of Iowa, Indiana, and Minnesota with "river runs through it" campuses have added this women's sport and are rapidly increasing their competitiveness.

Women's rowing became a sanctioned NCAA varsity sport in 1997. With the "christening" of the sport and the raised level of Title IX, women's crew has created a whole new opportunity for young women athletes across the U.S.A.

On May 14, 1999, an article appeared on the front page of *The Wall Street Journal*. The article verified the impact of Title IX gender-equity rules in college athletics and

CHAPTER 1 WANTED: FEMALE ATHLETES 5'10" AND TALLER

emphasized that each NCAA Division I women's rowing program could offer twenty full scholarships or equivalent partial scholarships. With the scholarships available, universities went looking for talent. As head coach for Michigan State in 1999, Bebe Bryans recruited one of her best rowers, an ex-swimmer, right out of the campus population. My daughter, standing six feet tall, attended a crew meeting after seeing a campus flyer that read: "Wanted: Female Athletes 5'10" and Taller - Born to Row, But Don't Know It Yet."

When I asked Stacey Hicks, M.S.U. Freshman Rower of the Year in 2000 and all-Big Ten 1V8+ First Team Stroke honoree in 2004, how she got interested, she told me her dad showed her *The Wall Street Journal* article. She was instantly intrigued about the sport.

In my four years as Novice Crew Dad, often I would hear the comment, "A non-rower took up crew because she couldn't make it in her chosen sport, usually swimming, cross country, track or sometimes basketball or volleyball." From my observation, nothing could be further from the truth. With the skill set, strength, endurance, and overall conditioning required, I would reply to that comment, "You've got to be kidding me," or "Put that person on a rowing machine (erg) and see how long he or she could last!"

Although the opportunities have increased, not every tall, athletic female can make it in this sport. The most likely to make it are the athletes who are used to the grueling self-discipline of aerobic training. Swimmers and runners are usually in that category. My daughter played basketball and volleyball, but was able to develop the discipline and mental commitment to the training demanded of crew. As she stated, "Crew is no easy sport. We gave everything we had in practice to get the results we wanted on race day." At her first meeting, over two hundred females showed up. After a couple of practices, that number dwindled quickly, but still left opportunities for a total of sixty women.

I interviewed Krista Buzzell, a former track and cross-country runner who "walked on" the team. She went from a non-rower "walk-on" to an all-American Stroke in her four-year career. When I asked her to describe the success factors, she replied, "Determination, persistence, support from teammates, coaches, parents, and a competitive spirit." At 6 feet tall, with broad shoulders and muscular structure, Krista was blessed with an ideal rowing body. She combined her physique with an incredible work ethic, and an all-American academic status, to become a real role model for crew. Krista exemplified the true spirit of a student-athlete at a Division I university.

1.2 Over 5'10"
Krista Buzzell, Kirsten Seif, Stacy Hicks

With the increase in demand for female rowers, more interest is being created in clubs and high school programs. This, along with the enhancement of collegiate programs, will not only improve the caliber of crew, but also raise the level for the U.S.A. in international and Olympic competition.

A T-shirt I purchased for my daughter spells out "tongue in cheek" the Top Ten reasons to row:

1. I have nothing else to do at 5:30 a.m.
2. After working out twice a day, I get drunk faster.
3. The port-a-johns at regattas are always a treat.
4. By wearing the same clothes over and over, I save money on laundry.
5. I like pulling on a long stiff shaft.
6. "Constructive" criticism from my coach is good for my self-image.
7. Catching crabs while rowing is preferred to catching them other ways.
8. I want a small person with a Napoleon complex screaming and spitting in my face.

9. I like having an excuse for blisters on my hands.
10. I like the circular marks the seat leaves on my butt.

Man vs. Woman

Women's rowing began to flourish with both increasing numbers of universities emphasizing coeducation and a growing general acceptance of women participating in sports. I remember when I was in high school in the mid sixties, there was a girl who had a better basketball jump shot than most guys. At the time, however, she was looked down upon and ostracized by both the boys and the girls, almost as if she wore a "scarlet A" on her sweater. Timing in life is everything!

In rowing, the physical effort, techniques, and equipment are exactly the same for women as for men. Women can train like men without physically becoming men. Most varsity collegiate rowers range in height between 5'7" and 6'2", and vary in weight between 140 and 185 pounds. Females are usually sensitive about their actual weight. However, the pounds issue cannot be ignored in crew, as it determines the placement in the boat and acts as a measurement of how much a rower can pull versus her weight. If a female athlete doesn't apply every ounce of strength to move water, she could be viewed as the "anchor." Obviously, this is not a desirable nickname in this sport!

Rowing equipment is virtually identical for women and men. Because women are naturally lighter than men, often the rigging (oar configuration) is set with the oar point closer to the blade of the oar to decrease the angle of the lever, making it easier to pull. In addition, the riggers are pitched lower than for men to allow for less height in women. The foot-stretchers are also adjusted to the sliding seats to make up for women's shorter legs. Also, now there are hull classes designed for the average weight of rowers in a shell so women's shells may have the same design as the lightweight men. Some manufacturers even make women's shells slightly wider to accommodate wider hips of the female anatomy. Except for these equipment adjustments and minor differences of the shell, the sport of rowing is exactly the same for women and men. The entire cycle of the stroke, from catch to recovery, is equal, regardless of gender. (See terms in CHAPTER 3, *Know Your Row*.

With not only the acceptance, but also the endorsement of women in sports by today's society, women's crew has accelerated in popularity. "Wanted: Female Athletes 5'10" and Taller" has become a great ad and the calling for motivated women athletes who want a challenging sport.

CHAPTER 2

Women's Crew Surfaces

As the boat master strikes his mallet on a block, alternating the cadence, two hundred slaves row a warship for the Roman Empire in the Oscar winning classic, *Ben Hur*. The actor, Charlton Heston, plays number 41, a slave who manned an oar to the sound of the mallet for over three years. The scene in the movie is brutal, as chained oarsmen are being whipped to increase their stroke rate to obtain battle speed, attack speed, and finally, ramming speed. The commander cries out to the oarsmen: "Hate keeps a man alive; it gives him strength. All of you men are condemned, and we keep you alive to serve this ship. So, row well and live."

This scene is not recommended to inspire your daughter to try intercollegiate rowing. However, after she has rowed for a few years, I am certain she will be able to understand the emotion, and identify with the physical effort portrayed in the movie. She may even see in her mind the cox as the condemning master and think dreaded thoughts in the last 250 meters of a sprint. Watch the scene after your daughter has rowed awhile, because it is not for the faint of heart and is in the category of "don't try this at home, kids."

A Brief History

The fact remains that rowing started with these slave ships to move commerce and fight enemies during the times of the early Greeks and Egyptians.

The activity was further developed by the Romans and Vikings, two societies with a great spirit of adventure, who took to the seas for exploration, protection, and survival. As time marched on, rowing was perfected by the English, where it began as a sport with the first Henley Royal Regatta taking place in 1839. The River Thames is now the site of this famous regatta held annually in Oxfordshire, England.

There is a great chronology on the "Friends of Rowing History" website, www.rowinghistory.net. For example, the sport of women's rowing was first organized in 1893 in England, and was known as the women's collegiate "boating society" at Cambridge's Newnhason College. Although not really considered a ladylike sport at the time, women's rowing got its start, and was imported to the U.S.A. shortly after the inauguration at Cambridge. American women's crew started on the East Coast in 1897 with the Sedgeley Club, a Philadelphia Club for women rowers. The sport then jumped to the West Coast when the Pococks, a family of boat builders, moved to Seattle, Washington. They established roots with the University of Washington in 1899. Men's rowing was extremely popular in the early 1900's, and crew teams, like college football teams, were willing to travel across the country to compete. The events drew thousands of people to watch the competition.

Women's rowing gained popularity in England during the 1920's and 1930's with the first women's Head of the River race held on the Thames River in 1930. The Philadelphia Girls Rowing Club was founded by Ernestine Bayer in 1938, but the sport never really got traction in the U.S. until 1964, when the U.S. National Women's Rowing Association was founded. The first championship was held in 1966 over a 1,000-meter course. Following in 1967, the Philadelphia Girls Rowing Club sent the first U.S representative women's eight and a women's four to the FISA Championship.

The FISA is the Federations International des Societies d'Aviron formed in France in 1892 as the first international amateur sport governing body. The International Rowing

CHAPTER 2 WOMEN'S CREW SURFACES

Federation was moved to Lausanne, Switzerland during World War I to be based in a neutral country. The Federation governs the sport of rowing worldwide, manages its development, and is empowered by its members of National Rowing Federations and National Olympic Committees, as well as the International Olympic Committee (I.O.C.).

The "French Connection" to this international sport involves Paris born Le Baron Pierre de Coubertin, a very active sportsman and rowing enthusiast. In his 1928 booklet entitled, *Cures of the Oar*, he described the value of rowing for good health and teaching usefulness. According to Le Baron Pierre in this writings, "The oar is the ideal discipline." He founded the International Olympic Committee and established the first modern day Olympics, held in Athens, Greece in 1896. Le Baron Pierre brought rowing to the world's stage by making the sport an inaugural Olympic event. All the commands were in the French language and served as the origin for the words "petite," "grand" finals, and "repecharge" seen in today's rowing vocabulary. These words remain as the "French connection" blended with numerous English commands to make it a true international sport. (SEE CHAPTER 3, *Know Your Row*).

To summarize the history of rowing: the Egyptians invented it; the Romans developed it; the English perfected it; and, the French brought it to the world competition. Now, it is up to the Americans to take rowing to the next level, and it is happening for women with enhanced intercollegiate programs.

Title IX Enactment

The high water mark for women's collegiate rowing in the U.S.A. came in 1972 with the passage of Title IX. Title IX of the Education Amendment Act is a federal law that prohibits sex discrimination in any educational program or activity that is a recipient of federal funds. It states, "No person in the United States shall, on the basis of sex, be excluded from participation in, be denied the benefits of, or be subjected to discrimination under any educational program or activity receiving federal financial assistance." This Act applies to almost all colleges and universities, public and private. For the private schools, most are covered under the Act because they receive federal funding through federal financial aid programs used by their students. Title IX covers three issues regarding athletics. The first issue requires that women be provided with an equal opportunity to participate in sports (defined as sports in which they are interested). With the growing interest in women's crew and the numbers required for a team, rowing allows a college to more closely equalize the participation by both women and men in a sports program. The second issue requires that female athletes receive athletic scholarship dollars proportional to their participation. The last part of the Act specifies equal treatment in all the factors surrounding the sport: equipment and supplies, scheduling of games and practice times, travel and daily allowances, access to tutoring, coaching, locker rooms, practice and competitive facilities, medical and training facilities, publicity and promotions, recruitment, and support services.

In conjunction with the Act, investments throughout many NCAA universities are being made in crew to make the sport for women one of high caliber. Practice times need to be equal to any other major sport, and it necessitates equality in all the facilities to make the sport viable and competitive. There has been a lot of controversy about the Title IX Act, especially around the "proportionality option." Many argue that ratios in sports should not have to be equal to the ratio of male to female undergraduates because not as many females are interested in sports. I would ask, "Says who?" Having two daughters who played sports in their childhood, I was very pleased that both of them got a chance to participate at the college level. To comply, universities can satisfy the intent of Title IX by demonstrating a continuing practice of program expansion for females over time. Proportionality does not have to be met immediately.

A May 28, 2004 *New York Times* article entitled "Rowing Scholarships Available. No Experience Necessary" by Juliet

Macur, reiterated the call for female rowers to satisfy Title IX requirements. Because of the number required for a varsity crew program, the demand far outweighs the supply and offers many opportunities for female athletes.

Club Sport vs. Varsity Status

As a Novice Crew Dad, I learned first-hand the difference between a club sport and a Title IX-sanctioned varsity sport. My oldest daughter, Lindsay, joined the Club Crew Team at Penn State University and served as our family catalyst to the sport. Not only did she train and compete, but she had to raise the funds to make crew happen. She and her teammates would "hawk" soft drinks at PSU football games, as well as run the concession stands. With scarce funds of a club sport, the team would solicit members to drive a car stuffed with rowers to each regatta. Once there, they would pile as many people as possible into a hotel room to stretch the funds. The equipment was comprised of hand-me-down wooden boats with oars painted by the rowers, all stored in a wooden shed in the summer and in the basement of the football stadium in the winter. Training was just as rigorous, but the team had "third world" conditions compared to a varsity sport. The club team practiced in Rec Hall where the exercise room also served as the PSU crew office. The team was the only crew that spent more time training on land than on water, mainly due to a lack of lakes and rivers in State College, Pennsylvania. The practice lake at Stone Valley was only 750 meters long, and by the time the cox called out the team's best effort, a "Power 10," the team was at the end of the lake and had to turn around. This was the routine when the lake was not frozen. Only dedicated club teams would drive to a training camp in South Carolina at spring break, sleep on bunk beds in unheated cabins, push a Suburban down the road for strength training, and wait for a layer of ice to unfreeze before beginning the practice.

Rowing at Penn State with the status of a club sport brought out the true adventure and spirit of competitive athletics. These conditions represent many club sports at universities across the U.S.A., and no matter the sport or gender participating, the teams face the same "equal" rights and challenges.

Contrasting a club sport with that of a sanctioned varsity sport is the difference between a mahogany shell and one made from carbon fiber. The Title IX Act has given women a chance to enjoy the value of a sports program, ultimately providing them with the opportunity to learn and understand the meaning of competition in a controlled and supportive environment. The combination of the full enactment of Title IX and exposure of the sport in publications like *The Wall Street Journal* and the *New York Times* has led to the surfacing of women's crew in its varsity-sanctioned form.

2.1   Penn State Club Crew 1998

Established as an official NCAA sport in 1997, and combined with not only the passing, but now the complete realization of Title IX, the sport has grown inward from the East and West Coasts to number 143 college teams across the U.S.A.

The scene of Charlton Heston chained as a slave to his seat contrasted to a scene of collegiate rowing with its sleek and clean competition venue, positions women's crew at a new civilized level. After your daughter has competed, watch the scene in *Ben Hur* and you can laugh and recall one of the first good news/bad news jokes: the commander of the slave ship announces he has good news and bad news. "First, the good news; all the oarsmen will be treated to a full course meal of all you can eat steak and lobster."

CHAPTER 2 WOMEN'S CREW SURFACES

A thunderous cheer goes up from the galley of slaves. Then the commander says, "Now for the bad news, the emperor wants to go water skiing!"

Women's crew has surfaced across the nation as a viable and respectable activity through which females can channel their competitive focus. Its popularity continues to grow, assuming, of course, that there is no water skiing emperor around!

CHAPTER 3

Know Your Row

Raised as a "Michigander," and now living in Cleveland, Ohio in the land of Ohio State Buckeyes, I became very knowledgeable about the traditional collegiate sports: football, basketball, and baseball. With the most knowledge of basketball, I enjoyed coaching my son and two daughters through 8th grade CYO (Catholic Youth Organization) competition. When my son got cut in his first year of high school basketball tryouts, I am the one who cried! My son said, "Don't worry Dad, I'm going to play Lacrosse." I asked, "What the hell is Lacrosse?" My son replied, "It's better than football; not only can you knock someone down, you can hit him with a stick." My reaction: "Oh, great!" Once my son started to play this game, invented by the North America Indians to prepare warriors for battle, I began to understand the sport by getting to know the terms, the moves, and the strategy in order to intelligently view the games.

In Lacrosse, it was just as important to understand "cradling the ball" as it was to know a "blitzing linebacker" in football, a "low post" in basketball, or a "squeeze play" in baseball.

The same situation existed for me in women's crew. To understand the sport, you must understand the terms, the intricacies, and the philosophy of rowing to really enjoy the competition. As a Novice Crew Dad, it took me all four years of my daughter's eligibility to soak up the terminology to be in the "know of row." Knowing the subtleties and the terminology will not only make you a better spectator; it allows better communication with your daughter, her teammates, and coaches. When you say, "Hey Kirsten, great squaring the blade for clean catches," your daughter will look at you the way your son did in Lacrosse when you said, "Great over-the-head check on the attackman by the crease."

This chapter deals with crew from stern to bow. It is a quick glance to "know your row" so you will be able to carry on an intelligent conversation with the coaches, or be able to understand the Sunday breakfast talk at PJ's Pancake House in Princeton, New Jersey before the great head race event, "The Princeton Chase."

Know a "Head" from a "Sprint"

There are basically two types of races in rowing: A "head" race and a "sprint" race. A head race is normally held in the fall season with competition held on a lake or river covering a distance of approximately three miles. I first thought that a "head race" was named after the source, the beginning, or head of a river. However, I quickly learned that it is a "race inside your head" where boats are staggered, have a running start, and race against the clock to see who has the fastest time in their class. These races serve several basic purposes. College coaches use them to improve techniques, build confidence, and keep the teams motivated as they go into the winter months. It is valuable water time especially for the "ice teams" like Michigan State where they are forced to train indoors when the lakes and rivers freeze, usually from late October-early November through February of the coming year. Water time is key for skills, timing, and motivation before the women hit the erg and weight machines indoors. Head races are also used to establish a name for the school's program. Winning head races in the fall creates exposure for a particular college team and helps to gain prestige and attract qualified recruits, serving to bolster a winning tradition. More descriptions and some popular head races are described in *All In Your Head,* CHAPTER 9.

The sprints are the races that capture the true competitive spirit of collegiate rowing. Held in the spring season, these races are side-by-side and head-to-head, over 1-1/4 miles. The standard race starts from a dead stop, and competition ranges from dual meets to conference and NCAA Championships with as many as six boats going oar-to-oar. Competition at the conference or NCAA level involves progressive heats similar to track and swim meets. The sprints are what the sport of women's crew is all about, where competition is keen, the racing is exciting, and where young women develop into fierce competitors. The sprints are the events for which collegiate coaches and rowers live. *Sprint to the Finish*, CHAPTER 10, describes the races in more detail, with insights into some key events.

Know Imperial and Metrics - Weights and Measures

Started by Egyptians, developed by the Romans and Vikings, popularized by the English, and modernized by the Olympics, crew has the mixture of imperial and metric dimensions.

Key Conversion		
Metric		*Imperial*
1,000 meters	=	.6214 miles
1 meter	=	3.281 feet

The race distances are all in metrics for Olympic and world competition. A head race ranges from 5,000 to 6,000 meters (3.1 - 3.7 miles) and sprint races are 2,000 meters (approximately 1-1/4 miles). In the U.S., reference to the boats and participants are all in inches and pounds. The length of an eight-woman-plus cox shell is around 58 feet; a 7/16 inch combination open/box wrench is used for rigging; and the minimum and best weight for a female coxswain is 110 pounds.

Know Your Terms

For a quick reference and understanding of women's crew, I have divided the terminology into categories. These categories will assist the Novice Crew Dad for easy reference to "know your row."

The terms are divided into the following categories and descriptions:

Category	Description
The Female Rowers	The people in the boat
All About the Shell	Boat terms from stern to bow
Winter Training	Ergs and tanks
Spring Training	Seat races and tapering
Racing - A Dad's View	A view from the shore
Racing – A Daughter's View	A view inside the shell
Inside Crew	Boathouse phrases

Along with the technical definitions, I have added my own Dad's Crew Cuts to the matrix, giving my own insight and interpretation from a Novice Crew Dad's perspective.

The Female Rowers		
Term	Definition	Dad's Crew Cuts
Coxswain (cox)	Person who steers the boat. Key course strategist 8+ (cox in stern), 4+ (cox in stern or bow, depending on boat design). Normally small in stature	"On the water quarterback." Emotional and intellectual leader. Knows physical and mental state of crew at all times.
Stroke (8th seat)	Rower that leads the rest of the boat; closest to stern; sets the boat's rhythm	Franchise player; like a star running back in football. Combines brute force with intellect.
Seats 7, 6, 5, 4, 3, 2	Seat positions between stroke an bows	See Chapter 4 "Every Seat Counts."
Bow (1st seat)	Rower farthest from stroke and closest to boat bow ball	Her stroke usually dictates the boat's overall balance. A graceful stroke and quick hands are key. Alone in the bow, she entertains herself.
Novice	First year rower in collegiate competition. Depending on team's depth, experienced rowers may be on the novice team their first year of college competition	Novice athletes are usually freshmen.

CHAPTER 3   KNOW YOUR ROW   19

Varsity	Collegiate rower whose skill is either more advanced than a novice or has completed her first year of college competition	Dedication and passion dominate these athletes.
Lightweight	A female rower 130 pounds and less	Found more in teams on East Coast that have long established programs. Many men's programs have lightweight categories.
V8+	Varsity eight crew consisting of eight rowers and one coxswain	Higher up on the competitive hierarchy, the V8+ races provide the most points for a team.
V4+	Varsity four crew consisting of four rowers and one coxswain	Sometimes the V4+ makes or breaks a collegiate program. Usually lighter rowers with a lot of heart are in these crews.

All About the Shell		
Terms	Definition	Dad's Crew Cuts
Shell	Rowing boats made from carbon fibers. 8+ boat weighs about 200 pounds	Getting into one is harder than it looks – don't step on the hull (fiber section) or your foot will go right through the shell.
Bow	Forward section of the boat; first section to reach where the boat is headed	In most cases, a 4+ cox lays flat within the bow in order to reduce wind resistance and lower the center of gravity.
Bow ball	First part of the boat to cross the finish line in a race	Based on a photo finish to determine the order of bow balls crossing the line, my daughter's crew has both won and lost races with a photo finish. It is THAT close.
Deck	Part of the bow and stern that completes the boat. The deck separates the rowers from the ends of the boat.	Deck-length lead often announced during the race, meaning that one shell has pulled away slightly from the rowers in the other shell, with about a 3 seat advantage.
Stern	Rear of boat; rowers face the stern	In the 8+, the cox ducks down in the stern to reduce wind resistance while viewing each rower's oar and direction of the shell.
Seat	A removable part of the boat on which the rower sits. It slides to allow for rower stroke and boat glide.	Seat rollers and tracks are often wiped in order to ensure a smooth glide while rowing.

Terms	Definition	Dad's Crew Cuts
Oar	Used to drive and balance the boat	On cold days, pogies (hand warmers) are used to keep the hands nimble and warm on the oar handle.
Rigger	Metal triangle support bolted to the side of the boat; allows oars to pivot from "catch" to "finish" (entry and removal of blade from water). Some riggers attach to the top sides, angling outward from the shell and are referred to as "wings."	My daughter learned about rigging using a 7/16-inch combination open/box wrench.
Gunnel	Upper edge of the side of the shell.	No gun mounts needed – this sport is hand-to-hand combat.
Blade	Hatchet-shaped part of oar used to propel the boat forward	Blade colors and design are the best way to identify your team on the water.
Oarlock	Attached to the rigger; locks the oar in place during rowing	Pressure on the oarlock is very important to the balance of the boat.
Button	Wide collar on the oar; keeps the oar from slipping through the oarlock and into the water	My dry-cleaner always destroys these.
Foot-stretchers	A resting place for the rower's feet within the boat; laced shoes usually are bolted to this	"Break a leg" in skiing; "Break a foot-stretcher" in rowing.
Rudder	Thin piece of material on the bottom of the stern that steers the shell	It's amazing how small the rudder actually is!
Stroke or *Speed Coach ™	On board "computer" recording times every 100 meters	Closest thing to an instant replay of a race
Cox box	Head set used by coxswain to communicate with team members in the boat.	High tech megaphone

* Speed Coach is a trademark of Nielsen-Kellerman Manufacturers

CHAPTER 3 KNOW YOUR ROW

Winter Training		
Term	**Definition**	**Dad's Crew Cut**
Ergometer (Erg)	Indoor rowing machine for training technique, strength, and endurance	My daughter fondly referred to the erg as the "torture machine."
Split	A measurement of effort; the split shows how long it is taking a rower to row 500 meters	Every erg workout usually has a target split for the rower. I am sure my daughter still remembers her best erg split, as well as her worst!
Rating – strokes per minute	Along with the split, another number shown on the erg as rower is rowing. Shows how quickly she is going up and down the slide.	A lower rating means a slower pace up the slide; higher equals a quicker pace. This measurement is also very important on the water.
Piece	Another word for an erg workout (also used on the water to reference each segment of the workout)	Pieces are usually no piece of cake!
Tank	Indoor rowing practice equipment; used to practice techniques	Video or mirrors are used to give rowers instant feedback on how they look during the stroke. "Rowed to no where."

Spring Training		
Term	**Definition**	**Dad's Crew Cuts**
Seat racing	By switching one rower in each boat and then racing, coaches can compare one rower vs. another	Some rowers and Dads do not understand this; coaches do.
Taper	A technique used by coaches to conserve energy for a big regatta	Used in swimming, distance running, and other high stamina sports to reduce the amount of training and conserve power for a championship race.

Racing – A Dad's View		
Term	**Definition**	**Dad's Crew Cuts**
Regatta	Rowing event where several crew teams compete	Sprints are the most exciting.
Head	Fall races "inside" your head - Length ranges between 5 and 6 kilometers	Colleges use for tune up for the Sprints.
Sprints	2000 meter college competition "2K" - common lingo	Exciting, especially with 6 shells head-to-head.
Sweep rowing	Each rower has one oar	NCAA Championship "Rowed to the Sweep 16."
Sculling	Each rower uses two oars	Usually single or doubles - not used in college competition, but is an Olympic event.
Grand Finals	Top six boats from the heats	A chance for a Gold, Silver, Bronze and most points in spring competition.
Petite Finals	Boats that usually don't finish #1 or #2 in their heats	Team points awarded but not normally a medal round; NCAA Championship first and second places now get 7th & 8th place medals.
C Finals	Boats not making the Petite	Row for pride – rowers call it the "truck". Not making the Grand or Petite makes you feel like you were run over by a truck.
Repecharge "rep"	French word for second chance for those crews not advancing automatically to the Grand Finals	I finally used my two years of high school French.
Race time	Total time elapse to complete race course	Times are variable, depending on head and tail winds, weather conditions, current, and race strategy to win or conserve energy for repecharge.
Stroke Rate	Strokes per minute used by the team: 45-50 at start, 36-40 middle of race, 40-45 sprint to the finish are common rates	This number is indicator of activity, but higher strokes do not ensure greater speed. Announcer usually keys in on the rate.
Open Water	A phrase meaning that one boat has completely passed another boat – so much so that there is water in-between the two	Open water is what every rower strives for as they race.

Racing – A Daughter's View		
Term	**Definition**	**Dad's Crew Cuts**
Bucket rig	Two rowers on same side next to each other not port/starboard alternate	Only saw this in V4+; usually done because certain rowers follow each other better than others. Also helps boat go straighter.
Stake	A person who holds the boat at the start	Used in most Sprint races.
Aligner	Person on shore or in a boat who makes sure all boats are even at the start	On shore at the Windermere Classic, uses a rope to align the boat.

CHAPTER 3 KNOW YOUR ROW 23

Term	Definition	Dad's Crew Cuts
Starter	Person who controls the start with voice commands and flag	Key person to ensure fairness. Works closely with aligner.
Hands up attention	Bow and cox use hands in air to signal not ready	Cox has power to not start if hand is up and not ready.
Attention	Call before go	Attention position of rower is crucial to power of the start - typically includes sitting up tall, straight, but relaxed arms and eyes straight ahead.
Run	The distance that the shell moves through one stroke	A good run is smooth with synchronous speed.
Stroke (four parts)	A complete cycle of a rower moving the oar through the water – 4 parts equal a stroke	Yelling: "Stroke-stroke" is not recommended- too obnoxious.
1. Catch	Oar blade drops in the water	Clean catch implies no splash; catching together as a crew is essential to speed.
2. Drive	Pulling the oar blade through the water	Power comes from the legs to drive; "Push off your foot-stretchers."
3. Finish	Oar handle is moved down, lifting the oar blade out of the water	Key here is feathering or turning the oar blade from vertical to parallel with the water; position where catching a crab is most common.
4. Recovery	Hands first, body slides forward for next catch	When I tried this, it looked like I was swatting flies – referred to as skying, oar too high off the water.
Feathering	Using the hands to turn the oar blade	Bow position must have quick hands to follow the front; should not use the wrists, just the finger pads.
Squaring	Hands rotate the oar perpendicular to the water	Great squaring equals clean catches. Oar goes into water like a knife through hot butter.
Settle	After the start, team settles into a rhythm; usually 38 to 40 strokes per minute for V8+	This is where you look for the smooth, synchronous motion; rowers strive to find a rating that will make them as powerful as possible without losing any control.
Swing	Engaging the back with the legs on the drive. "Opening up to the sky." Rowing looks smooth and effortless	Team is going like a bat out of hell.
Crab	Oar blade is thrust into the water at an angle and gets caught under the water	Painful (and usually frustrating)! Checks the boat (stops it from moving). An MSU rower was thrown out of the boat during a race against University of Michigan on a cold windy day at Lake Ovid after "catching a crab."
Port	Left side of boat	Port and left have same number of letters.
Starboard	Right side of boat	My daughter loved starboard – left hand in-board, nearest the blade.
Slide (full ½, ¾)	Seat slides on the rail	½ start to ¾ to full for power.
Power 10	Call by the cox for the team's best strokes with most drive	Good coxswains time these at the right moment for maximum gain.

Term	Definition	Dad's Crew Cuts
Lactic acid	A result of anaerobic threshold being reached. The goal is to delay the onset of LA for as long as possible. Rowing programs train for this delay	Bumper sticker reads: "Tripping on Lactic Acid."
Slump	Rower folds over after crossing the finish line in exhaustion	Have seen several rowers regurgitating over the sides.
Way-Nugh	An order given by either the coach or coxswain that means stop rowing, "Way enough.".	There are disputes on how this is actually spelled and pronounced (especially for novices).
Check It Down	An order that means all rowers square their blade and place it in the water; stops the boat completely	A little less painful than stopping a boat via a crab! Crucial with short distance after finish.

Inside Crew		
Term	Definition	Dad's Crew Cuts
Erg queen	Rower with the best time on the erg machine for 2000 meters and 20 minutes	Usually gets labeled "rowing animal."
PR	Personal record	Rowing or erging for a personal record is a great self accomplishment.
Crewmors	Rumors on a crew team	Naturally evolve with 60 women on a team.
Track bite	Bruises or marks on the back of the calves from scraping the slide	Marks on the legs are a crew fashion statement.
Rush the slide	Too quick to advance the seat, causing boat hesitation (aka, rush the seat)	Rush the seat in the Midwest is a 40-yard dash to the outhouse.
Bi-sweptual	Ability to row on the port or starboard side "like a baseball switch hitter"	Not to be confused with bisexual.

A working knowledge of the seven categories of crew will make you "the intelligent Crew Dad." No longer will you have to pester the coaches or your daughter before a race. The coaches will be able to concentrate on set-up, strategy and techniques while your daughter focuses on pulling her weight. Everyone will be better off when the Crew Dad is in the "know of row." Memorize these terms, and through your knowledge, you will graduate from Novice to a Varsity Crew Dad.

CHAPTER 4

Every Seat Counts

Now that the standard rowing terms have been addressed, the major component, the rowers themselves, need a little explaining. There are approximately sixty women participants who compete on a collegiate rowing team: two novice four-boats, two novice eight-boats, two varsity four-boats, and two varsity eight-boats. Including coxswains, the total is fifty-six women, along with a few alternates. Before we go into the role of each position within the program, let us first touch upon the role of the various shells. As mentioned, there are boats of eight rowers and boats of four rowers for competition. There are also pairs and singles. These all work to build success of the program in different ways. For instance, pairs and singles are mostly used for practice, in which the women athletes learn and re-learn technical skills such as balance. My daughter recalls several times when the athletes were broken down into twos in order to brave the water in smaller shells. When in a smaller shell, the imperfections of technique cannot be hidden. Smaller shells allow rowers to determine what stages of the stroke are hindering the quickness of the boat the most. If a pair or single is used as a technical practice, it won't bring on the sweat and fatigue of a four or eight-boat workout. Some of the top programs use pairs and singles for seat racing (SEE CHAPTER 6, *Spring Forward*), and then the intensity of the practice is turned up, and so is the sweat eq uity! There is a time and a place for both types of workouts on the water.

Eights and fours, or boats with either eight rowers or four rowers (along with a coxswain) are closer to the heart of the program, considering the fact that these two shells are ones that compete throughout the nation. These shells become the homes of the rowers, day in and day out. Although there is sometimes a shift of a rower from one side to the other, typically rowers become accustomed to row port or starboard. These shells make up the majority of the practices that test not only the technique, but also the endurance and strength of each athlete. Pieces are determined by the coaches and are usually comprised of a set time and rating that the boat must row to their maximum. A practice on the water could be comprised of as many as 10 or 15 separate intense pieces.

Obviously eights are the longest shells in the rowing program. They require the largest number of athletes and the most equipment. Although there is still only one coxswain, there are eight rowers working together to propel the boat down the racecourse. A program usually has a first and second (or "A" and "B") eight, the two top boats in terms of potential regatta points. Because these are the top boats, they are usually made up of the top performing athletes either on the erg or via seat racing.

Even though the eights get all the attention, a championship caliber team must have successful fours. Think of the saying, "A team is only as fast as its slowest rower." While fours usually house the athletes who do not meet the physical standards of the eights, they sometimes dictate the overall success of the program. The rowers in the fours create that natural tension to push the women in the eights to be better and drive the whole team's competitiveness. Like the eights, there are typically both first and second fours. In the fours, though, only the 1V4+ boat is eligible for NCAA championship competition. The fours are shorter than eights and the coxswain is positioned either in the bow or stern of the shell. In most of the four boats I witnessed, the cox was in the cox seat in the bow of the boat creating less wind resistance. In 2002, the four from Michigan State finished fifth in the nation. The crew of Stacey Atkinson, LaToyia Bowman, Heather Underwood, Erin Robertson, and cox, Stacia Beiniks, led the team to the second highest finish of all boats in school history. Overall, the team finished ninth in the nation in 2002 with a solid performance. In my opinion, look at the fours when trying to determine the success and ability of a program.

A Football Comparison

In every team sport, each position on the squad is essential to both the quality of performance and the final outcome of competition. In no other sport have I seen the critical dependence of each member working in unison as I have witnessed in rowing. Regardless of the boat configuration, each rower represents a necessary piece of the puzzle. Although each seat position has a personality, a style, and a talent all its own, a single rower, for best effectiveness, loses individualism to form a blend with fellow teammates to create a synergy.

Most dads like me are familiar with the game of football and know the types of players required for all eleven positions. Each position, from offensive lineman to quarterback, has a unique physical attribute as well as certain personality traits that characterize the skill level and mindset required. A pulling guard is usually quicker and more agile than an offensive tackle. A quarterback needs leadership ability as well as unique ball-handling skills and speed. Watching a football game, most fathers keep a close eye on the offensive guards to predict the type of play that is unfolding. When the ball is hiked, the guard's blocking schemes develop run or pass plays and usually telegraph the direction of that play. In fact, many defensive linemen will study the stance of the offensive guard. A subtlety such as the color of fingertips will reveal the play about to happen. Because they have played the game or studied it, dads have learned all about the players and the strategies of football.

28 W CREW - STROKE TO BOW

4.1 V8+ makeup
Shell with "wing" riggers

Know the Seats - V8+

To better understand the sport of rowing, it is also important to know the seat positions in the boats. Each seat has a given set of skills, responsibilities, and character traits essential for the best team makeup. A look at the heart of the program, the V8+ shell, bow to cox, illustrates the variety of positions. For easy identity, I have given each seat a name befitting the character and role each plays in the shell.

Starting at the bow (front of the boat), "Blanda Bow" and two seat "Talise Two" are the bow pair who must be totally in sync. The togetherness required of these positions reminds me of the same precision timing needed for football wide receivers to run their pass routes. Timing is critical for football "wide outs" to be at an exact spot when the ball is delivered. Balance to catch the ball, especially with two feet in bounds at the sideline, is an extremely valuable skill. In rowing, the bow and number two seat require this same grace and harmony to make sure the boat is balanced. Symmetry is the skill set needed for the pair "sitting" bow.

Bow "Blanda Bow"

Blanda, Latin for "smooth and seductive," as the bow rower has the role to steady the boat. She is dependable and loyal to the team and her boat. Often she possesses an effervescent personality because she sits alone in the front of the boat with only one teammate as a talking partner. The crew can rely on her for a joke to relax the team in a tense situation. Being chatty, Blanda will blurt out a technical comment to improve the crew's skill, or make a couple of expletives to inspire. She has the best view of all oars and can make adjustments based on what she sees and feels inside the shell. If the boat is not set, look at the level of Blanda's hands as she moves up the slide, for the balance of the boat is in large part a result of her movements, especially her arms and hands. I was particularly fond of M.S.U.'s fun loving and boisterous 1V8+ bow seat, Katie Isaacs, from Buffalo, New York. Katie, a 2004 all-region second team honoree, fit the bow description so perfectly that if you looked up Blanda Bow in the World's Rowing Dictionary, you would see her picture!

2 Seat "Talise Two"

Talise, a North American Indian name meaning "lovely water," is in the two seat and completes the bow pair. Her ability to balance the shell creates the "lovely water" situation. She also teams up with Blanda Bow to supply the needed sense of humor, especially at the all-intense start of a sprint. Talise Two and Blanda Bow are "partners in rhyme".

Maintaining balance and grace are critical. Think of Blanda and Talise as girls on a seesaw. If one girl is heavier, or in this case, is putting more weight on the oar handle, the shell tips to one side. They must be completely level with one another in order to give the shell equal height in the water.

The next four seats of V8+ are the 3, 4, 5, and 6 positions referred to as the engine room of the shell. These are the four seats that normally comprise the tallest and strongest rowers. I deem these positions as the "offensive linemen" of the team. They possess the strength and endurance to power the boat, just as the guards, tackles, and center provide the grunt work to make a football play successful. Like the offensive line in football, these middle seat positions on a crew team are the unsung heroes.

3 Seat "Thelma Three"

Thelma, a Greek name meaning "will," occupies the three seat and exudes more energy than anyone else in the boat. The cox usually will have to yell to calm her down and focus, as she is oftentimes the life of the shell. In certain instances, she is also the "transport," or the athlete who switched from another shell, and comes with the will and determination to make her contribution effective for the whole crew.

4 Seat "Farica Four"

Farica, old German for "peaceful ruler," rows four seat and rules the bow four rowers of the boat. Her concentration is centered on following the stern four as she makes sure that the seam of the boat does not rip. Think of her as the glue holding two moving pieces together and the challenge and importance of her role as the peaceful ruler can be respected.

5 Seat "Faline Five"

Faline, Latin for "like a cat" purrs in the five seat position, serving as the hub of the engine. She has the feeling of movement all around her, making her the central core of the dynamic unit. Her power must be matched by control and smoothness, like a cat ready to pounce on her prey, as the shell "leaps" from its start.

6 Seat "Serilda Six"

Serilda, old German meaning "armed warrior women" fills seat six and is all power. She has the stern pair ahead of her and can usually see Cadence Cox's eyes just above the stern pair's shoulders. Her position is critical to transfer the stroke rhythm to the rest of the boat. Because of the importance of conveying the rhythm, some coaches rate the six seat almost as important as the stroke. Regardless, no one doubts her ability and willingness to pull hard, armed as an oar warrior.

Probably the most critical seats for a coach to fill are the stern pair. These two have both the power and rhythm of great running backs. Just as great running backs have the ability to power up the middle or cut to the outside with breakaway speed, the 7th and 8th (stroke) seats have the strength and control to lead the team to victory.

Just as an all-American running back scores touchdowns and is in the limelight, the stroke is hailed as the "franchise" rower in the shell. She normally has the best rowing physique and is usually a mixture of intellect and animal. Her title of "erg queen" of the team usually fits perfectly. Behind her in the 7th seat is the understudy of the stroke and would compare in football to the blocking back. A blocking back is usually called upon to pick up a first down in a crucial yardage situation, but seldom gets in the record book for the score. The 7th seat is like this back, critical to the crew's success, but without the glory of the stroke.

7 Seat "Swanhild Seven"

Swanhild, Saxon for "battle swan," is the no-glamour position of seat number seven. She battles every stroke and does it extremely well. She mirrors the stroke in each movement and leads either the starboards or ports, depending on the rigging formation. Because she is not first in line, she does not get the glory like Stella Stroke or the accolades like a star running back. In this sense, Swanhild is the living essence of the sport of rowing. Rowing gets very little glory, although it requires tremendous skill, strength and intellect.

Stroke "Stella Stroke"

Stella, Latin for "star," sits tall in seat number eight and is physically, emotionally, and mentally the leader of the shell. The coxswain can say anything she wants, but if Stella Stroke does not react to her words, it is like rowing through molasses.

All the responsibility of the stroke translates to tons of pressure. Again, referring back to the football analogy, you can often find the coach huddled down in discussion with Stella Stroke, analyzing how to run the plays for the best "scoring" opportunity.

The 9th seat is the coxswain whom I refer to as the "quarterback" of the shell. The quarterback in football is the team leader from both physical and mental standpoints. In crew, the cox is small in stature, like a jockey. Her physical attributes are relegated to steering the boat, which is crucial to keeping a "true" course and not losing precious fractions of a second in a sprint race. Most of the cox's quarterbacking skill comes from the mental and emotional area. Just as the plays in football are sent in from the sidelines, the cox must implement the strategy in stroke rate, timing of moves, and power sets. In addition to carrying out the strategy, it is up to the coxswain to know the ability of each rower and extract the most energy out of the team as a whole, all in the right moment of a race.

In my opinion, many races are won or lost by the "call" from the cox to position the boat during the first 1,500 meters and to start the sprint to the finish. All this adds up to having the mental capacity to know the strategy, the team, and the competitive situations. Her emotional leadership must generate the most power from each rower and the highest energy from the team collectively.

Cox "Cadence Cox"
Cadence, Latin for "with rhythm" breathes life into the shell, literally through her voice and directionally through her aiming of the shell down the racecourse. She must be able to read people and cater to their needs. Oftentimes, this is done through instinct and is very spontaneous. She must know how to react in every imaginable situation, from hailstorms to open water blowouts to photofinish endings. In order to have a fast crew, no one can doubt her ability to do these things.

From Blanda Bow to Cadence Cox, the nine women of the shell are all in it together, from the time the flag goes down to the time the horn sounds at the finish. My daughter rowed mainly in the starboard engine compartment (three and five seats) and was the "battle swan" in seat seven for part of her career. No matter the seat or the side, it is up to all eight rowers to become one under the direction of the cox. Extracting every ounce of energy from the body over approximately seven minutes, they leave everything they have on the water.

4.2   Seat Positions V8+

Know the Seats - V4+

A "four" is just a smaller version of the standard eight boat, operating similarly with ports and starboards, bow and stern. However, the skills and personalities of each of the four rowers, as well as the coxswain, can sometimes vary from the standard eight. By condensing the skills and personalities needed in the eight rowing positions, a four encompasses women who can multi-task. By no means am I stating that eights do not require this as well; however, the need becomes more acute as boats shrink in size.

For example, the stroke must not only be a strong leader in terms of control and pace, but also a great listener. "How are the other three rowers responding to me and my movements?" and "What do they need from me in order to row this boat properly and at its greatest speed?" are common thoughts of a stroke. Because the shell is more intimate, the more accomplished stroke can better understand the needs of the boat and how these rowers respond to her actions.

Seats two and three fill a unique role unlike the engine room of a standard eight. This is because these seats are part of a bow or stern pair as well as being the core of the boat. Again, these rowers must fulfill multiple tasks in a four in order to succeed.

The bow seat's responsibility is heightened in terms of balance. The level of her hands throughout the recovery is in direct correlation to the balance of the boat. As in the eight, she has the vantage point similar to the coxswain in that she can see all oars throughout the drive and recovery and can, therefore, account for a balance flaw with her own actions. She must be both reactionary and powerful. However, in the four, she also can take on the responsibility of communicator. This leads us to the definition and role of the coxswain in a four-man shell.

The coxswain is usually positioned in the bow of the boat, tucked snugly underneath the deck of the shell. Most shell manufacturers design the cox seat in the bow because in the four-boat it is more efficient to push the lead weight than to pull it. The front cox provides less drag from wind resistance, and with fewer rowers than an eight, the boat can be monitored safely. The coxswain views the water ahead and relies heavily on the cohesiveness of the rowers to manage the movement of the oars along with their own bodies. As the cox in a four, she must be able to "feel" the shell and diagnose any behavioral issues that may be hindering maximum speed. For instance, the oars hanging at the catch may cause a quick stop of the boat's progression. A slight checking or hesitation of the boat could be due to a slow release at the finish. She must also communicate with the bowman to understand the needs of the rowers, all while trying to steer the boat correctly.

All in all, rowers in fours are not that different from rowers in eights. However, their actions, emotions, and skills more immediately affect the boat and its speed. They must be flexible, and deal with the "feel" of the boat on a stroke-by-stroke basis. Because fours make you react to the overall feel of the shell, as well as allow you to enhance your various rowing skills, often coaches will have all team members practice in fours.

No one can deny their effectiveness in team bonding and skill building. Just like all other members of the team, rowers who compete in fours are an integral part of the overall varsity program.

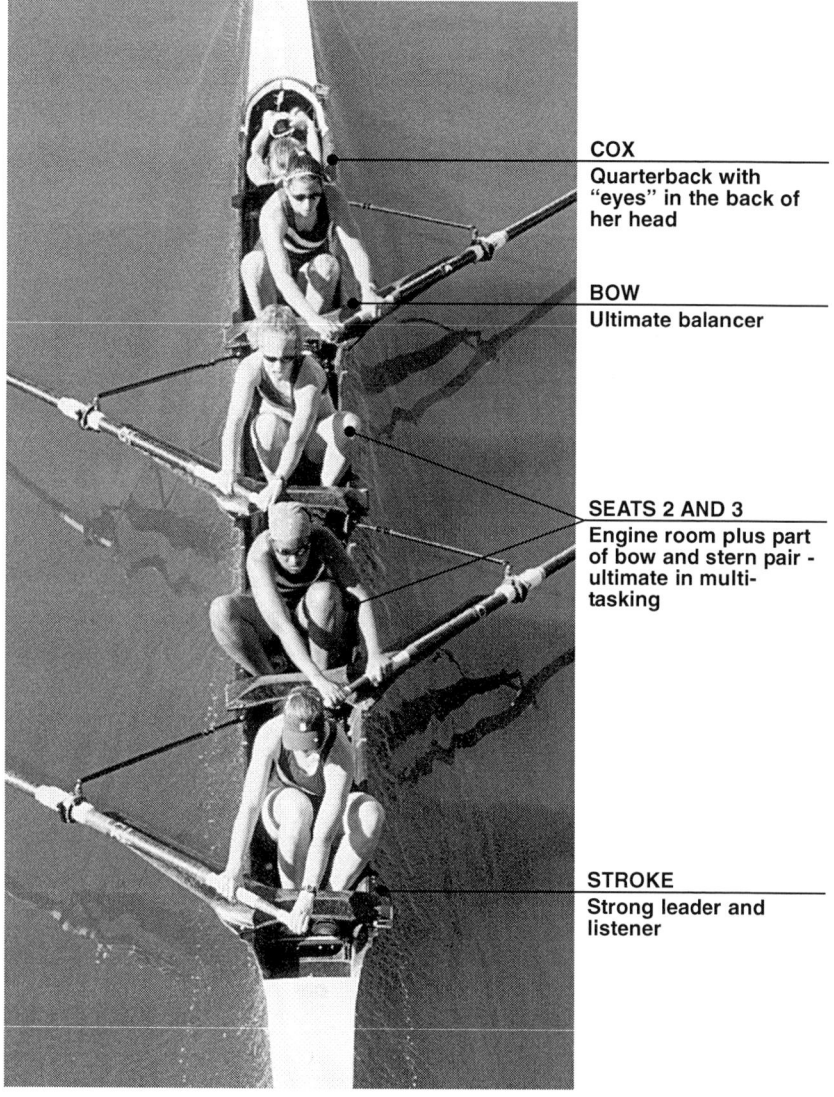

COX
Quarterback with "eyes" in the back of her head

BOW
Ultimate balancer

SEATS 2 AND 3
Engine room plus part of bow and stern pair - ultimate in multi-tasking

STROKE
Strong leader and listener

4.3 V4+ makeup
Shell with "wing" riggers

Team Chemistry

There is a lot of talk in sports about a team's chemistry. Crew chemistry is defined as the physical, intellectual, and emotional interactions between the rowers that affect the overall performance of the team. When the natural tension of competing for a specific boat or a seat position is positive and friendly, the chemistry is good. If, however, anger and frustration exist between rowers, it may cause internal conflict.

4.4   Emotional bonding before a race

This could lead to a disruption of a team's synergy, ultimately resulting in slower speeds. As you can imagine, there are many human interactions in a team of sixty women. Constant monitoring of politics by team captains and coaches is done to keep the false rumors (nicknamed "crewmors") from spreading and positive energy flowing.

Crew requires a special bond physically and emotionally to create synchronous motion. It is for this reason that rowing, like no other sport, depends on excellent team chemistry to achieve greatness.

Port vs. Starboard

In a V8+ shell, the coxswain faces the bow and has direct eye contact with the stroke. Facing the bow, the cox has the port side on her left with the right side seating the starboard rowers. For the landlubbers like me, I always remember left is port and right is starboard because port has fewer letters than starboard as "left" has fewer letters than "right."

Whether your daughter rows port or starboard is often determined by the side she learned to row or by the dexterity of her hands and comfort in body coordination. To paraphrase, Daniel J. Boyne in *The Red Rose Crew*, {It is as difficult for rower to row from both sides as it is for a baseball player to be a switch hitter.}

In baseball, the weight distribution and hand techniques are very different for a left-handed hitter vs. a "righty." The same is true in a crew team of port vs. starboard. The key to this understanding is in the function of each hand. The oarhand (in-board), closest to the water, is the primary hand for feathering or rotating the oar between the horizontal and vertical positions during the stroke cycle. Feathering requires excellent dexterity with the right hand for port rowers, and with the left hand for women rowing starboard. With the majority of the population being right-handed, many women can more easily manipulate the oar with their right hand. The opposite hand is positioned closest to the end of the oar handle (out-board) and is used to leverage the oar and power it through the water. In addition to the hands, the body goes through a slight twisting motion that is coordinated with the stroke action. The port rower reaches the left side of her body forward and over to the port side of the gunnel while the starboard rower does the same toward the starboard side. This weight distribution and twisting motion may also feel better on one side of the shell vs. the other. It is this comfort level of hands and body that is a learned technique, and with many rowers, it becomes "natural" with the side on which they originally trained. Some coaches try to teach rowers to row from both sides, and the ones who are "bi-sweptual," add more value to the team just as switch hitters increase the versatility of a baseball team.

In the end, the side on which your daughter rows does not matter. She will experience the same sets of triumphs and challenges. Coaches seat each woman rower to maximize her technique, power, and balance in order to achieve the greatest efficiency and speed. The matching of the individuals to a particular seat is not only a function of a person's skill set and character traits, but is also a function of how well they mesh with the person in front of them. There is no denying that each seat in the boat plays a key role to the shell's collective stamina, and mental and emotional toughness. Every rower must be kinesthetic, having a complete sensation of full body movement. The saying, "We are all in this together" describes the situation perfectly; every seat counts.

CHAPTER 5

The Big Commitment

It was winter break of her freshman year and my daughter pulled the car up the driveway to unload her suitcases. In the backseat, nestled with her pile of laundry, was an erg machine. Weighing only sixty pounds and split in two pieces, was a Concept 2 erg machine borrowed from the coach. Right then and there, I realized that rowing had one intense training schedule where you could not let up for one day. The Bible teaches us about the "law of use," use it or lose it. Determined to "use it," my daughter did not want to go one day without a "row to the max" erg workout so she could be ready for the upcoming winter training in Florida. That's when I, as the Novice Crew Dad, realized that the collegiate sport of women's crew was a full-time engagement. My daughter was imbued with the big "Commitment."

With the level of competition in all collegiate sports today, it is rare that a student athlete can participate in more than one sport or anything else besides her studies for that matter. An NCAA sport is a full-time job, and every seat does count in a rowing program, making each athlete's level of commitment to preparation that much more important. Rowing is no different than any other varsity program, as it is a year-round sport involving development of the cardiovascular system and muscle groups that require both endurance and strength.

Although nothing is novel about that, the thing that makes rowing unique is the way in which rowers prepare for competition. Many times, rowers are limited to practicing outside of their competition environment due to Mother Nature. Most upper Midwestern schools have about three to four months of winter that freezes all water. Fog, wind, ice, and snow usually, although not always, leave the crew "waterless." There are instances where coaches choose to battle the elements in order to get some necessary water time, having shells carve channels in the layer of thin ice or navigate cautiously through clouds of heavy fog. However, the ergometer and weight room are back-ups to the open water. In fact, most rowers will agree that racing on the water cannot be done as effectively without the strength and conditioning aspect of rowing, which includes both erging and weight training.

The Big Erg

Rowers can row inside, no matter what the outdoor conditions, using the ergometer, also lovingly referred to as the "big erg." The erg machine forms the basis of winter training in the parts of the country and the time of year where there is inclement weather. Typically between November and February, teams huddle indoors, training their bodies and minds in great anticipation of being on the water. During this time, the erg becomes not only the mechanism for strength and endurance training, but also the dreaded machine of mind games and muscular pain.

The machine itself is almost an exact simulator of rowing movements. Have you ever seen an erg collecting dust in the far-off corner of the gym? Although it is not the most popular cardio machine at the local gym, its importance is measured in gold to a hard core rower. There is a value, trust me. Rowers can get both lessons in technique as well as pulling effort from ergometers. Just like a cycle machine in a gym trains bikers in technique, strength, and endurance, the erg machine trains rowers. Obviously the "feel" is not entirely the same from erg to water, since you do not get the glide of the boat, or the catch of water sensation on your oar. But when weather is a rowing obstacle, or when an athlete chooses to work out on her own, the erg is an essential tool.

CHAPTER 5 THE BIG COMMITTMENT

Rowing machines were developed for training back in the mid 1800's. They were difficult to use and did not clearly simulate the technique or conditioning required in the shell. The early 1960's gave birth to the ergometer. The main components of the machine are the chain, resistance flywheel, handlebars, seat, slide, and foot-stretchers. Older renditions tend to look more like fans, while state-of-the-art ergs have a more sleek appearance. A resistance chain wraps around a wheel up front, so when a rower pulls on the chain via the handlebars, the force of propelling the flywheel simulates the force of propelling the boat forward on the water.

Everything else, the seat, slide, and foot-stretchers are pretty much identical to those found in the shell. As my daughter has told me, the erg allows her to do a hell of a lot of work and go nowhere. Sounds like fun to me!

One of the most popular ergs that is found in crew training rooms at universities is the Concept 2. The machine, designed by the Dreissigacker brothers in Morrisville, Vermont, has gone through several developmental iterations to simulate rowing and provide a benchmark for performance. The latest models come with computer performance monitors situated directly in front of the rower's face, calculating every stroke. The monitor shows the distance equivalent rowed in meters, the stroke rate per minute, the time elapsed, and the 500-meter split times.

Rowers on the erg get immediate feedback on how hard and effectively they are pulling each stroke. As you can imagine, this allows for a stressful environment when erg tests and crucial pieces are being performed. This is especially true when teammates and coaches are right above your shoulder watching (and judging) along with you.

When my daughter set up the erg machine in our basement over Christmas, I hopped on to get a taste of this torture. As I started, my daughter began to howl with laughter as my technique looked like something out of a bad disco movie. She labeled me a YMCA rower with uncoordinated leg, arm, and back movements.

Just like rowing on the water, the correct erg motion requires muscular engagement of legs, arms, upper torso, and back. With the proper motion, correct body coordination can be simulated and practiced. In addition, aerobic capacity for distance, along with training for short bursts of power, simulating a Power 10 maneuver, can be enhanced.

Usually, once every three to four weeks, the coach sets a time for erg tests. All teammates anticipate these tests with great anxiety. Because definitive numbers are established at each test, coaches can determine not only the performance of each individual, but the overall competitiveness of the team. Performance numbers as well as a rower's desire to improve show up in the erg times.

Erg Strategy and Times

Coaches evaluate each rower's overall time for completing the 2000-meter distance in order to measure improvement and positioning within the team. Splits, times to row 500 meters on the erg, are viewed as a standard benchmark in rowing, similar to football coaches comparing the 40-yard dash times between players. The most common strategy for an erg test is to start off fast, 40+ strokes per minute, to make the first split of 500 meters the fastest. Then, the erg rower settles in at 35 to 36 strokes per minute

5.1   Erg Room - Princeton Boathouse

making the second and third splits, the third and fourth fastest respectively. The closing split simulates the sprint at around 40 strokes per minute to make the last 500 meters the second fastest split time.

The split is dictated in large part by the rating, which is a number typically between 18 and 36 that illustrates the rate a rower is pulling. The higher the rating, the quicker she is moving up the slide and going around the catch. The higher rating usually means that the split is coming down as well. If it is really low, such as an 18 or even 16, she is going slower up the slide. In most instances, a lower rating means a slower split; however, this relationship of rating to split is dependent on the rower. Some women produce better splits by keeping a rating low and the slide very controlled. Coaches will often talk about ratio, which is referring to the time up the slide versus the time pulling. By having a good ratio, or a big discrepancy between the two parts of the stroke, the split typically will come down. This means that the rower is adding more speed to the boat. As long as the ratio is good, rowers tend to show good splits that ultimately result in decreased time it takes to pull a certain number of meters.

As hinted at earlier, the erg is not supposed to be enjoyable. Instead, the erg is used mainly to simulate not only technique, but the pain experienced by rowers in a race. Usually about 1,000 meters into a race, pain and muscle fatigue are at a peak. Without practicing the way in which to deal with this pain both mentally and emotionally, rowers lose their edge. The erg allows athletes to practice reacting to physical pain and overcoming it. By having the time, splits, and rating directly in front of you stroke by stroke, the progression of the workout cannot be ignored. The rower cannot escape the erg cycle, just like she cannot take a mental hiatus in the shell during a race. Instead, she must focus on driving that number (split) down and producing more speed. Once she does overcome that pain produced on an erg, it can be one of the most empowering feelings an athlete can encounter. It is mentally and physically equivalent to the distance runner's "high."

The difference between split times is usually small with no more than four seconds between the fastest and slowest splits for first class indoor rowers. To follow this strategy, the splits would look something like this for a 7 minute, 12 second, 2,000-meter time:

	1st 500m	2nd 500m	3rd 500m	4th 500m	Total
Min/sec.	1:46.2	1:48.6	1:50.2	1:47.4	7:12.4

I picked this time as it was my daughter's personal record (PR) when she was rowing in the "engine room" (seat 5), averaging a 1:48.1 split time. She also received the honors of "erg queen" for being in the team's top ten best overall time for the erg exercise. As a comparison, the stroke's time overall time ranged from 6:58 to 7:02, making the average split time 1:44.5 to 1:45.5. In collegiate women's rowing, the total time for a 2000-meter erg is estimated to be between 6:50 and 7:50 for competitive V8+ and V4+ athletes.

As a reference point, in Boston, Massachusetts, the World Indoor Rowing Championship is held every year. In 2002, the Women's Open was won in a time of 6:30.8. For the macho dads, the World Indoor Record is held by Rob Waddell of New Zealand with a time of 5:39.5 for a 2000-meter indoor erg sprint. Now that's kicking butt!

Although the erg does not exactly simulate water rowing, the erg test does represent a consistent comparison that can be replicated as a world standard. Coaches do use these tests to help identify seat position and boat assignment. At some schools, the first thing asked of new a recruit is, "What are your erg scores?" As a Novice Crew Dad, I never knew my daughter's erg times, nor did I have enough knowledge to ask. Other programs might have their rowers sit down and perform an erg test before they are even welcomed into the new rowing year.

Despite the fact that erg times are performance indicators, the actual water sport requires much more skill in controlled motion and power to be successful. There is no penalty for mass on an erg machine, but body weight to pulling force ratio is the key parameter when sitting in a shell on the water. I once saw a T-shirt that read: "Put an erg on the water and it sinks."

Erg times and regatta times are performance predictors, but do not tell the whole story. Times achieved in a regatta do not mean a lot because of the variables in wind conditions (head and tail), weather, and water currents. However, rowing was meant for the water and much more skill is required in an 8+ woman shell than pulling a handle on an erg. The erg and its times are relative indicators, but should be taken as the machine suggests, "in concept."

Rowing/Erging Through the Pain

Observing my daughter and her peers over four years, I would sometimes ask myself: "Are oarswomen pure masochists, or are they truly conquerors of physical and mental thresholds related to their own bodies?" Although there is pain from normal injuries related to backs and knees, the greatest pain and pain anticipation is the overtaxation of body exertion causing lactic acid burn. This symptom is realized in all situations where high repetitions of muscle movements are combined with high endurance such as a marathon runner "hitting the wall" towards the end of the race.

During a race or intense workout, each rower can reach her limit of oxygen intake causing less flow of oxygen-filled blood to the muscles. The combination of muscle contractions and energy expense results in a body chemical reaction producing multiple metabolic by-products. One of these by-products is lactic acid. With less oxygen available for muscle contraction efficiency, less oxygen to discharge by-products, and an increased deposit of metabolic by-product, the result is a burning sensation. Lactic acid is known as the "acid of fatigue," and the muscle burn is extremely painful, known by all who participate in endurance sports. Rowers especially experience the increase of lactic acid production because the sport demands the use of all major muscle groups and most small ones.

Thresholds of pain vary by individual, but this "burn" must be endured more in rowing than any other sport because of the high dependency of the team on each person's performance. A rower's ability to keep expending energy, even when the needle on her "pain meter" is in the red zone, is critical or the boat will lose speed. Our 7th seat in the 1V8+ boat was Laura Thomas. Laura's facial expressions during a race were always the perfect picture of pain. She was a true battle swan who always gave everything she had which was expressed by the perfect grimace.

With the proper training, women can improve their cardiovascular system, increase the level of oxygen intake, and heighten their lactic acid threshold. The level of oxygen intake is referred to as VO2 max. A rower's fitness can be measured by the amount of oxygen in liters she can consume while exercising at her maximum capacity. Increasing the exercise intensity helps raise the VO2 max, which increases the stamina and raises the threshold to endure pain. The mean VO2 value in female athletes is 2.7 liters of oxygen per minute, which is about 25% less than the mean value for male athletes. As a benchmark, women competing in international competition have a minimum of 4 liters of oxygen per minute intake.

The big training commitment must involve endurance. Lactic acid burn is a part of the sport, and many times it is the impetus for meteoric anxiety before an erg test or a race. The rower knows she will be in pain! Erg tests, as well as certain races on the water, have been compared to childbirth. Being female rowers, it is often joked that they will be great moms giving birth since they know how to deal with the pain. The so-called beauty of both is the phenomenal fact that the most intense pain is forgotten once the child is born, or in this case, the finish line is crossed.

The Indoor Tank

Another indoor training tool is the use of a large rowing tank of water. Although the tank does not provide the feel of shell balance in the water, it does allow rowers to work on oar technique, stroke cycle sequence, rhythm, and style. As a hollow oar is swept through the water simulating a complete stroke, mirrors positioned next to the tank provide important critique. During the winter months, the tank is used approximately two times per week. In some instances, an established boat is seated to their positions to practice timing and harmony. In other cases, eight rowers are seated at random to help them improve their ability to mesh with each other. "Mirroring" the movements of one rower in front of another is a definite discipline. Tanks are a wonderful teaching tool for novices and can provide experienced rowers a chance to perfect their style in a team atmosphere or a solo workout.

Weight Training

The erg and indoor tank are not the only ways coaches train and prepare their rowers for competition. Weights add another component that can greatly increase the effectiveness of rowers within the shell. Weight training for women rowers concentrates on building powerful thighs and shoulders with lean forearms and calves. Strong quadriceps and buttock muscles deliver the major power to the rowing stroke. Typical exercises with weights include: squats, lunges, bench presses, and seated rows. Depending on the time of the year, the emphasis may be on heavy lifting or low resistance/high repetitions. The main goal is to keep building strength without building huge muscle mass. Muscle bulkiness can reduce flexibility and reach which are extremely important at the "catch" portion of the stroke. Too much muscle mass may also be a deterrent to speed and control of the oar.

Besides keeping strength at its peak, weight training can help build confidence and togetherness as rowers work in pairs and push each other to do well in the exercise. The weight room also becomes a center in which rowers congregate, builds "family," and enhances team unity. All in all, weight training is a positive force in developing a successful rowing program.

Health and Nutrition

My daughter's college experience was not just heavily influenced by the erg practices and regattas. To be a rower at the varsity level, preparation goes far beyond the physical exertion of practices and races. One facet of effective preparation is nutrition. Each rower has a different body type and each varsity program has its own level of intervention into the eating habits of the rowers. Some rowers are naturally smaller in stature and need to eat volumes of food in order to maintain muscle mass; others maintain muscle mass without any effort. Some programs avoid desserts the night before a regatta, while others permit rowers to have as much food as they want, including desserts, before racing. However, as in everything else, there are guidelines or common practices to which most programs adhere. For instance, foods provided at the racecourse or hotel before racing usually consist of fruit, granola bars, grains, and maybe yogurts. The idea is to consume very "light" sugars that can be burned quickly when racing. It is very rare for a rower to eat chocolate chip cookies or a piece of pizza before a race.

Another common best practice is for rowers to eat pasta with some sort of lean protein the night before a race. Most programs stay away from steaks, pizza, or Mexican foods the night before. Similar to the reasoning for eating fruit immediately before a race, pasta provides a very important energy source for most rowers. With that in mind, coaches tend to scope out Italian restaurants when traveling into a new area for the night.

Water is another nutritional "must-have" in rowing. Rowers can be found trucking around their water bottles, not only around practices, but also throughout the entire day. A very common habit is to place the water bottle in the back behind the uniform. Getting back to the effect of lactic acid on the body, water is the natural treatment for sore muscles, burning throat, or even the rower's cough. Without water or a sport-type drink, rowers can quickly become very dehydrated.

No matter what nutritional rules are in effect, one thing is for certain: throughout the training season (or in other words, the entire collegiate year), the act of eating is very sacred to rowers. It is not uncommon for rowers to become grouchy before dinner or even after practice because they are so hungry. There are probably girls on the team that are notorious for being hungry all the time, and the talk of food is on the list of favorite conversation points. Food takes on a life of its own within a rowing program. A close second is probably sleep.

Food and water are natural ways to prepare and replenish the athlete's body. There are, on the other hand, many regulations surrounding unnatural sources. Like every other varsity athletic program in the country, drugs are strongly prohibited. All rowers gather once a year to undergo NCAA training on its rules and regulations. Rowers are required to sign a drug form before they are officially considered a part of the team. As a follow-up to this form, random drug testing occurs once a week during the prime rowing season. Those that are found positive are then required to be drug tested in each following week. If there is another positive finding, the rower is suspended from competition.

Women's crew creates personal sacrifice like no other women's sport. This is due to the fact that, by design, conditioning puts the body through a cycle of pain unique to rowing. Reaching the physical and emotional limit in almost every erg practice, tailoring the body's intake of food, and surviving multiple physical ailments, demand from every female athlete one hell of a big commitment inside!

CHAPTER 6

Spring Forward

Spring Training - A Move to Water

As the ice on the water begins to disappear, the blood in a rower starts to quicken. She hears the trickling of the snow now melting into the lake and the birds chirping their first announcement of spring. Erg pieces, weight training, and tank work have been done over and over again to prepare the entire team for its peak season. Racing shells come out of hiding and are slipped into the water. Rowers are able to see nature around them as they row together. They begin practice on the water with enhanced endurance and strength, and revived spirits.

Yes, training on the water also occurs in the early to late parts of autumn; however, the intensity is so much greater in the spring months. Coaches' plans for each practice are calculated down to the last stroke and everyone is ready to "show their stuff." The NCAA caps the total time an athlete can spend on a sport at twenty hours per week. Each day of spring training normally involves two to three hours practicing on the water and one to two hours in other forms of conditioning, all keeping within the maximum hours allowed.

A time is designated when all rowers meet at the boathouse. This is usually in the morning, well before classes and sunrise. If the boathouse is not on campus, there may be a transportation system in place to get rowers without cars down to the boathouse every morning. Every program is different though, so your daughter may have an alternate way of arriving to practice each morning. Needless to say, traveling to practice involves long periods of silence as rowers have not entirely awakened (and probably won't until they feel the water beneath their shell).

Once all rowers are congregated together, there may be some land exercises that help to wake up both rowers and their muscles. Lineups for each boat are then called, and everyone gets their gear prepared for the next couple of hours on the water. This usually includes water bottle, socks (for the foot-stretcher shoes), hats, rain gear, hand warmers (pogies) if it's cold, and maybe even a roll of tape. The tape is lifesaving when new blisters begin appearing. It is important to note that usually the more seasoned rowers will not have as much of a problem with blisters since their hands have been callused with erg workouts and lifting, as well as rowing in the fall regattas.

In the boathouse, the coxswain will ensure that all her rowers are together before calling, "Hands on." This announces to the team that all rowers in the boat should have hands on the shell in preparation to take it down off the rack (or out of slings). The cox will then make many more calls directing the boat and her rowers to the dock. The shell is eventually rolled over from above the rowers' heads to the water in one smooth movement. Then, each rower opens her oarlock and grabs her oar, which has been placed down on the dock before practice begins. Once everyone is in the shell, the cox coordinates the team to push off the dock and navigate out into the open water. Practice on the water then begins.

A typical practice session on the water is comprised of warm-up, "pieces" or segments of intense rowing, some technical work, and cool-down. Depending on the comfort level of the boat, warm-up usually involves a rotation of pairs (8 and 7 seat, 6 and 5 seat, 4 and 3 seat, and bow pair - 2 and 1 seat) so that either 6 or 8 rowers are rowing at once at all times. A focus on basic technique gets everyone on the same page, while their muscles awaken to the stroke. The core of the practice on the water is obviously the intense pieces determined by the coaches. Varying in duration, rating, and sometimes even the amount of rowers rowing, workout pieces essentially train for racing. Mentally, physically, and emotionally, rowers start experiencing the elements of a race. By running down the body and mind, and finding a way to persevere through everything, rowers get stronger and more prepared for race day.

Technical training, although by no means as intense, is an essential component of practice. Not every day allows for this, but coaches usually make it an element of practice a few times a week. Plus, if you think about it, every stroke pulled on the water is practicing technique, whether designated a warm-up stroke or within a workout piece. The goal is to have the rower's muscles and brain "memorize" the exact elements of the perfect stroke. A quote from Vince Lombardi, the famous Green Bay Packers football coach, applies directly to spring training: "Practice does not make perfect; perfect practice makes perfect." Cool down is just as it connotes, a way of getting rid of lactic acid build up created during the time on the water. It is a time of team-building as well. Rowers are analyzing the success of the pieces and the overall feel of the boat. Sometimes, there are even some smiles for a job well done.

Seat Racing

Unfortunately, finding the most effective rowers in a boat is not an exact science. There are so many factors that play into the speed of a boat and what a rower can bring to that boat. Excellent technique, pulling their own weight (or more), leadership, and heart are all contributors. However, coaches must make decisions. A way to help in this decision-making is through seat racing.

A phrase that causes uneasiness and anxiety in rowers' stomachs, "seat racing" focuses on one rower in each shell. Two boats line up side-by-side and race a determined distance. The time for each shell is recorded. Then, the boats position themselves right next to each other so that two rowers can switch. Once the rowers are in place within opposite shells, the boats turn around to the same starting point and race the same distance again. Those times are then recorded. Based on time as well as overall look of the boat's rowing, coaches can determine the effectiveness of each rower that switched. For instance, if Sally from Boat A switched with Sue from Boat B, and Boat A had a time of 4:30 and Boat B had a time of 4:45 before they switched, the times after they rowed again would show whether Sally and Sue made the other boat go faster. Let's say that Boat A had a second time of 4:20 and Boat B remained the same, Sue would have won the seat race.

It is not a faultless system. This is because seat racing is based on the assumption that all rowers in each shell will row with the same intensity and effectiveness in each race. However, sometimes a rower will lose a seat race because someone in her new boat was having problems with her stroke, or was not pulling as hard as she did before. Hence, seat racing is a bit subjective. However, it does allow the competitive nature of the rowers to emerge.

Hand, Back, Knees, Head

The pain in rowing does not just last the length of the racecourse. There are many signs that these rowers are in pain well after they leave the shell or erg. In the main body regions, certain ailments may have to be endured. Trainers attend to the skin, muscle, and joint conditions of a women's team.

Don't be alarmed when your daughter shows you her hands. The manipulation of the oar handle (feathering) causes friction and creates sores and blisters. Ointments, Epsom Salt soaks, gauze, and tape are the normal remedies with the oarswomen who fight through the discomfort until calluses are formed. The touch and feel with the hands on the oar is essential to control the oar movement and maintain balance through proper height and angle.

Back pain can also be common. With the bending and twisting motion, the lower back can become stressed, and care must be taken to avoid lower lumbar disc problems.

The proper exercise, stretching, warm-up, and rest can help to strengthen the back muscles and eliminate back discomfort. Most team trainers supply heating pads to athletes with back discomfort about a half hour before practice or racing. This helps to loosen up the muscles for activity. Then, after rowing, trainers usually supply ice in bags to place on the sore back. Normally the team will bring a training table to the regattas, and the trainer works with the women to stretch out important back and leg muscles.

Knees and hips are also vulnerable injury areas. Each stroke cycle in rowing involves the equivalent of a leg press, and women can demonstrate real power as they try to "break the foot-stretchers." The constant motion of the coil and uncoil leg press can tax both the hip and knee joints. Strength exercises, such as barbell squats, develop the quadriceps, gluteus, and hamstrings to increase muscle mass and protect the working of the hip and leg joints.

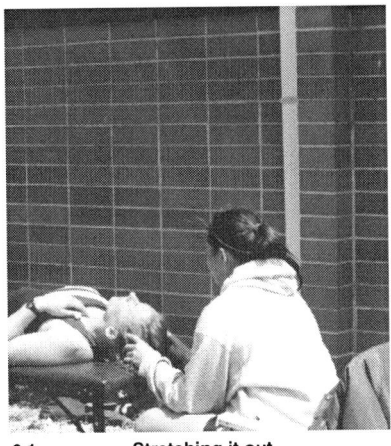
6.1   Stretching it out

The other "H" part of the body is the head. No physical injuries occur here, but there can be headaches that come from over-exertion or oxygen deprivation. Often, when I would see my daughter at regattas, she would have a consistent cough. I labeled that as "crew cough" that comes from burning lungs irritated through intense exercise. Don't be concerned, as the whole team coughs in rhythm. They are not ill, just hardworking athletes.

Lactic acid can affect a lot more than just the throat and lungs after a race. I have heard of muscle cramps and extreme fatigue after races. This can be so extreme that rowers will lie down and physically not be able to get back up again without much effort. A way to combat this is to continue drinking plenty of water or water containing electrolytes.

Making It Fun

Amidst all of the hard, laborious practices on the water, there are appropriate times for some fun. Usually this is at the end of the competitive season, or within the tapering period of training. To taper is to reduce one's use of energy in anticipation for the big racing event. The hope is that by cutting back on the level of effort rowers exert at practice, their muscles have time to rest and prepare for maximum exertion in the future. During the actual race, the body's well-trained systems kick into gear after this rest period. Tapering, however, is not a strict science. Just like the subjectivity of seat racing, tapering factors into the picture with multiple issues. What is the energy level of the team? How important is the race? What level of intensity had the team practiced at immediately before the tapering period? How do the rowers respond to rest?

Coaches usually like to mix it up a bit on the water, and put some smiles on the faces of their team. Rowers themselves leap at the chance to relieve some of the pressure practice brings. Fun exercises such as "flying," switching ports and starboards, and even placing a rower into the coxswain position to steer the boat are just a few examples. Flying, in particular, involves the rowers swinging their leg up on top of the oar handle to steady the boat while their arms wave in the air like a bird. Of course this only works when the boat is initially going fast. Then on a call, all rowers replace their hand position with their leg. It creates an amazing gliding sensation.

To create team fun and laughter, in the fall, the Michigan State team would hold an inter-squad Halloween regatta. One year my daughter's boat won the costume contest. It was hilarious to see all eight rowers dressed like Australian animals with the coxswain as the crocodile hunter. No matter what the activity, these fun exercises are crucial to building team togetherness. Plus, smiling releases endorphins that ultimately boost an athlete's energy level. *Are we having fun yet?*

CHAPTER 6 SPRING FORWARD

Whether there is a grimace of pain or smile on her face, the spring season produces a rejuvenation of spirit for the female athlete. Seat racing and tapering alike have one end goal that is very near: sprint racing. For every rower who was meant to be a rower, the thought of racing brings on a sense of excitement like no other. Spring forward ladies, and dads, too!

6.2 Halloween - rowing "animals"

CHAPTER 7

It's a Shell Game

Although the guts of crew is all about the rowers who supply the power to propel the boat forward, rowing is a shell game. The shell is to the crew team as a stock car (NASCAR) is to its driver. In rowing, the shell and team become one integral unit physically as well as emotionally. In NASCAR, the driver is "molded" into place and is weighted and balanced in the car for maximum speed. There are many parallels in both types of racing, which will be discussed later in this chapter. Many crucial components make up the construction of a crew boat and need to be understood by the Novice Crew Dad.

Construction

Shell construction has advanced to a lighter, faster racing boat that cuts through the water. Up until the mid 70's, crew shells were mostly made of wood and crafted by traditional wooden boat builders. These wooden boats usually had an oak frame with thin strips of mahogany compressing the outside of the shell. They would glisten in the water and signify a mark of beauty. The appearance in the water is like viewing the old Chris Craft® mahogany powerboats that are very regal looking and have that traditional classy look. While beautiful, these wooden boats weighed approximately three hundred pounds for a sixty-foot, eight-man shell. Imagine that weight on your shoulders while carrying the boat, never mind propelling it through the water! Just as in all other sports, new construction materials emerged for equipment. The 1972 Munich Olympics gave birth to a new construction of fiber-reinforced plastics that revolutionized shell construction. The new material consisting of glass, carbon fiber, honeycomb, and epoxy resins created crew boats that are lighter, stiffer, stronger, and more durable. This new shell also required less maintenance than previous wooden construction. A carbon fiber, eight-man shell weighs approximately two hundred pounds. These lighter-weight shells were ideal as women's rowing emerged because they created not only easier portability, but better maneuverability in the water. The end result was better racing speed and agility.

On parents' day at M.S.U., the Novice Crew Dads launched the shells, ever so careful not to step on the unsupported carbon fiber shell and put our big feet through the bottom. With the new fiber construction, the word "shell" is really synonymous with "eggshell."

Shell Components

Although a coxswain might think that the microphone and speaker system is paramount in a shell, the components

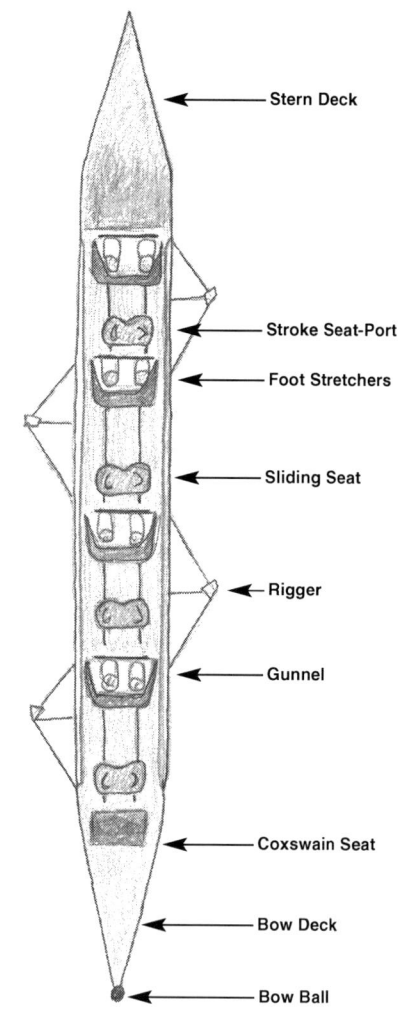

7.1 Four Layout

that make up the core of the racing shell are arguably the sliding seat, rigger, and oar.

Sliding Seat

The U.S.A.'s biggest contribution to the sport of crew is the sliding seat. Before these seats were invented, rowers wore leather on the bottom of their shorts and added grease to slide on the seat. J. C. Babcock of New York City is credited with the sliding seat concept in 1870 and was used successfully at a regatta in the Hudson Amateur Rowing Association. Today, a molded plastic or carbon seat is set on seat rollers consisting of nylon wheels mounted on ball bearings.

Great care is taken to ensure a smooth glide of the rollers along a stainless steel track to perfect the timing and power in each stroke. With the rower's feet affixed in laced shoes bolted to the foot-stretchers, a push-off with the legs transfers the power as the seat moves back. The seat slide is critical with the rolling weight inside the boat. In an eight-woman crew, all rowers combined, there is more than a half ton of rolling weight which is not contributing to driving the boat forward when the oars are out of the water. The entire team must have precision timing and not "rush the slide" or move too quickly to the catch, for fear of counteracting the shell's forward motion. When the oar blade drops in the water creating the catch, the sliding seat should stop and reverse direction without hesitation. Failure to do this will result in checking the shell, or producing a quick halt in the forward progress of the boat.

Someone on shore may notice this by a slight hesitation of the boat and even a pause in the oars before they hit the water. To maintain even a fraction of an advantage on the slide, many rowers will wipe down the inner groove of the slide to allow for a smoother glide. The difference is tremendous. It can feel like floating on air as opposed to gliding on sand. A good demonstration of how all components of the shell are intimately related, the success or failure of the smooth slide is sometimes best seen in the fluidity of the oar across the stroke.

The Rigger

The rigger (when referred to as part of the shell) is the metal framing that holds the oarlock. The rigger is constructed of aluminum or stainless steel that serves as the outboard of the shell and is bolted to the reinforced sides of the shell. There are also riggers that bolt to the top of the sides and transverse across the boat, then angle out to support the oarlock. These angled riggers are referred to as "wings." Based on strategy and team body composition, the coach adjusts the angle of the rigger and oarlocks with shims in an attempt to maximize the team's performance.

7.2   Rigging the boat

Part of the discipline of the sport is that each rower is expected to rig the boat before the race and de-rig the boat after the race, win or lose.

Oars

Just as you become attached to your favorite putter in golf, rowers become personally attached to their oar. The oar is an extension of their hands, transmitting every ounce of their body strength through the oar shaft to the blade in the water.

Oars have been traditionally made of wood. Carbon fiber, just as in shell construction, is replacing wood for lighter weight and more durability. Sometimes each rower has her own oar for the season and takes full responsibility for the care and maintenance. She may grease the button to provide smooth pivots in the oarlock. With full care of her own oar, she also ensures that the blade does not chip, which would cause a loss of efficiency. The handle of the oar is between 12 and 18 inches long, and its surface is key for gripping and feathering, especially as weather conditions change.

CHAPTER 7 IT'S A SHELL GAME 65

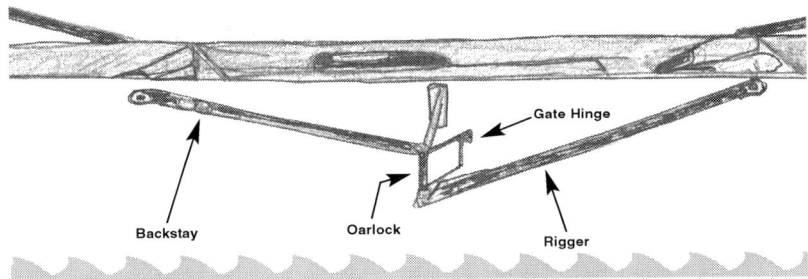

7.3   **Rigger and Oarlock**

In the cold regattas of the North, pogies or oar handle covers are sometimes used to keep the hands warm and flexible to manipulate the oar. You might be interested to know that pogies, when viewed in their most primitive state, are long tube socks with 2-inch cuts made on each side of the sock. The oar handle fits through these holes while the rower's hands are inside the socks. This allows the rower's hands to feel the oars without being exposed to the outside elements. Of course, you could go out and buy a stylish pair of pogies for those cold days, however, in the end, each type does the job.

Sweep oars are 12 feet in length and weigh approximately six pounds. Again, the weight is being reduced with the carbon fiber construction that can especially be a benefit at the end of a sprint to maintain control as fatigue sets in. The oar blade has changed over the years from a tulip or "Macon" blade to the modern-day hatchet design. The hatchet design is now more standard, providing added power and efficiency.

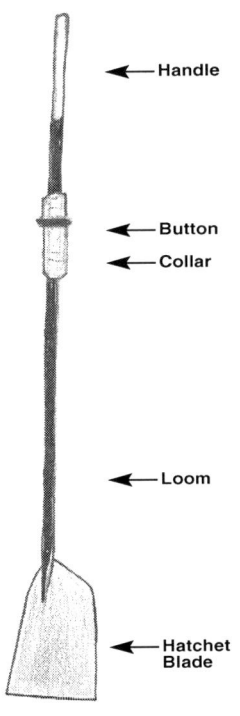

7.4   OAR

These three most critical components of the shell marry the rower with the equipment to maximize performance. In addition to the development of these components, shell manufacturers continue to improve the overall shell design through the use of new materials and technologies, all in the name of greater speed.

Shell Manufacturers

There are many manufacturers of shells located in the U.S.A., Canada, and countries throughout the world. From my observations, there are several American manufacturers who supply shells to the universities for their rowing programs. Each manufacturer has its own boat construction advantages and will contact the coaches to sell the benefits of their products and their company. The best selling method is to allow a team to demonstrate a shell before the sprint season starts to check out the features and benefits before making a purchase decision. Following, in alphabetical order, is a listing of prominent American manufacturers that I have seen:

Manufacturers	Location
Dirigo	Biddeford, Maine
Pocock	Seattle, Washington
Resolute	Warren, Rhode Island
Vespoli	New Haven, Connecticut

Coaches Equipment

In addition to selecting the boat configuration of shell, rigging, and oars to maximize the team's performance, the coach also utilizes other tools to increase speed and to analyze how to make improvements. Coaches will use a pitch meter, which is a level-like device, to determine the pitch of an oar. Pitch or angle of the oar as it enters the water is a key variable that each coach adjusts to maximize the power that each rower can generate. For practice sessions and races, the coaches will also analyze a team's performance by use of a "speed" or "stroke coach." The Speed Coach™ (trademark of Nielson-Kellermen) is a small electronic device that is attached to the bottom of the hull a set distance from the end of the bow. The device has an impeller that spins and is set proportional to the speed of the boat. The device records times every 100 meters and stores them electronically. Water current does affect the accuracy, but the device allows the coach to check each boat's game plan versus actual outcome. As the technology improves, many teams are trying new global-positioning instruments with increased accuracy. Boat technologies have come a long way from the old primitive wooden shells and heavy equipment used when the sport began.

Crew Parallels NASCAR

Those familiar with NASCAR (stock car) racing know that many standard specifications exist for the race car to promote even competition. All race cars must contain the same four 29/32" hole restrictor plates to keep the air intake equal, thus making the horsepower of the cars the same. In addition, thirty templates are used to ensure that the shape and contour of the bodies of the cars are aerodynamically equivalent. Also, there is a 3,400-pound minimum vehicle weight and a combined 3,600-pound minimum weight for vehicle and driver. All these rules are made by NASCAR to create as much parity as possible in the vehicle construction and weights so that the focus is on the drivers' skills and pit crews' abilities.

Even with all the rules and specifications, NASCAR race teams find ways to enhance their speeds by proper weight balance and other secrets and tricks that they can use to lessen the drag coefficients and improve track performance of the vehicle. One almost-folklore story in NASCAR is where a team cheated at the car check stand to reduce the drag coefficient. Teams want the car as low to the ground as possible, but NASCAR has a minimum car height when measured from the ground. One team designed the car below the minimum and at the test stand, designated one of the teammates to wear steel-toed shoes. They drove the car to the stand and onto the teammate's foot so the car would "make the minimum height." I have heard of cheating, but that was really taking one for the team. Also in NASCAR racing, weight distribution is one way to improve performance, especially as the races shift from various degrees of banked tracks. To lessen the weight of the car, teams would use hollow bolts to gain an advantage.

Weight is a crucial factor in rowing as well. In the Big Ten and NCAA Championships, each team's boat is weighed. There is a minimum weight of 205.03 pounds (93 kg) for each 8 plus cox shell, and just like the NASCAR and driver, there is a total minimum weight with cox. Again, for a 8+ shell, the minimum weight is 315 pounds with 205 pounds for the boat and 110 pounds minimum for the cox.

If the cox doesn't meet the weight, she must carry dead weight such as sand or other ballast. The dead weight must be located near her torso and cannot be distributed (unlike NASCAR) throughout the boat.

To my knowledge, the cox weight is the only parity rule that exists. The only bending of the weight rule I have heard of was when a lightweight cox drank as much water as she could hold before her weigh-in between one and two hours before the scheduled time of the first race of the day. This added weight was "released" after the weigh-in. The weight of the rowers vary, but it's up to them to pull their weight where all the rest of the boat and cox is considered "dead" weight. There is no set of standard specifications involving the shell design, and manufacturers continue to look for ways to improve performance.

In four years, I have not heard a peep about improving the performance of the shell itself, but perhaps team trade secrets exist, just as NASCAR tries to reduce wind resistance to gain an advantage. In rowing, the foreign substance rule states that "no boat shall have on its hull any substance that is water-soluble or partially soluble or that alters the mechanical or chemical interaction between the hull and water. There can be no use of bottom tape and only non-soluble varnish or paint can be applied." This rule stands, for all shells must be created equal.

CHAPTER 7 IT'S A SHELL GAME

In the sport of rowing, just as in NASCAR, it is all about the people and competition of the human body, mind, and spirit. Crew teams use rigging of pitch angles and proper weight distribution of the rowers themselves to achieve their best performance. Shell speeds depend on the strength, timing, and techniques of the crew, and a few pounds saved here or there probably do not make a huge difference. After all, it is the horses, not the chariot, that are important. Look for the competitive advantages in the rowers, even though it is a shell game.

CHAPTER 8

Every Race Has Its Course

One thing I learned in the fours years as a Novice Crew Dad is: If you've seen *one* racecourse, you've seen *one* racecourse. Unlike the built-in equality of a football field or basketball court, there is a wide variety of regatta courses for both head and sprint races.

Head Courses

The most varied are the courses for head races. These fall races are usually held on rivers with a course ranging from 5,000 to 6,000 meters in length. The layout and contour of these head races vary widely with maps of the course provided by the organizing committee to show launch areas, returning crew paths, and the racecourse itself, marking all turns and course obstacles. The U.S. Rowing rules restrict the types of turns. Turns of 180 degrees involving "spin" turns are not allowed, and changes in direction of the racecourse is limited to those that can be made under a normal racing pace with standard steering and oar power. The coxswain must be at her best to steer through course turns and negotiate bridge abutments, buoys, and other obstacles to minimize the distance traveled in a head course race. Plus, even in head races, there are usually a few neighboring boats themselves trying to navigate through the various obstacles. Sometimes the true challenge is coordinating movements between shells while also making sure to avoid time-consuming directional changes. I remember our team grazing a buoy at the Head of the Lake course in Seattle,

Washington. This increased the team's time and affected them mentally as they tried to focus on the rest of the race after the collision.

Sprint Courses

In "Rules of Rowing" for U.S. Rowing, there is an entire section describing sprint course requirements and certification. There are two major categories considered when evaluating a quality sprint course. The first category is overall weather conditions including both the prevailing climate and shelter from the wind. Regattas will happen through heat, rain, cold, snow, ice, and gloom of day. The two conditions which will "shipwreck" a race are lightning and high winds. I experienced both of these stoppages in my four years, including cancellation of a dual sprint with Notre Dame because of high winds; and also delays at the NCAA Championships in Indianapolis with dangerous lightning conditions. The best courses have good shelter from the wind to allow for safe conditions. There is no cure against lightning, high winds, or tornadoes.

Head races as well as sprints can be affected by weather conditions. In the fall of 2000 at the Head of the Ohio, the afternoon portion of the race had to be called off due to high wind conditions. High winds swept across the Three River area creating white caps and dangerous conditions. Several boats capsized and rowers had to be rescued from the chilly Pittsburgh waters before the race was finally canceled.

The second major category revolves around the water conditions to make a sprint race as fair as possible and safe for every young woman. The most competitive courses are free of current, or only have a slight current distributed equally across the racecourse. The banks of the course also need to be able to absorb the waves rather than reflect them back into the lanes, causing a ripple effect.

An unequal current condition is the biggest disparity, which can create an unfair advantage. Even mild currents in lakes, rivers, and reservoirs can be prominent in the middle of the body of water. The center of the course is where the winners of the first heat are positioned. These middle lanes (3 and 4 of a 6-lane event) could have slight water current advantages that may even assist a team in winning a race. The best courses have currents of less than one meter per minute and generate no unfair advantage across all lanes. Quality racecourses are also free of floating objects such as logs, which could make water conditions both unsafe and unfair. As my daughter has shared with me, there is nothing like having your blade slap down on a floating log to get the adrenaline flowing!

Sprint Set-up

As a Dad attending a sporting event where your daughter participates, you always want to know the set-up. The Novice Crew Dad needs to have an idea of how a course is layed out to understand how teams compete to win and how best to view the regatta. The end goal is to maximize the time spent watching the events involving your own children. The U.S. Rowing organization is a nonprofit membership organization recognized by the Olympic Committee as the national governing body for all U.S. rowing. This organization provides a course certification with Class A, B, and C, with the best courses receiving an A rating. These Class A courses make for the best events.

8.1   Course Start at Oak Ridge, Tennessee

The Class A sprint course is 2,000 meters long (1-1/4 miles) and wide enough to accommodate a minimum of six racing lanes spaced 13.5 meters (44.3 feet) apart when marked by a buoy system. A minimum of 5 meters (16.4 feet) between the shore and the outside perimeter of the course is required for a Class A rating. Also, the water is specified to be at least 3 meters (9.8 feet) deep throughout the course, and most competitive courses have room for return lanes and warm-ups.

The Start

The best courses have quality starting platforms or anchored stake boats so that the shells are held stationary and "true" for a fair start. An aligner's station is positioned on the side of the course and is equipped with a vertical wire aligned with a target on the opposite shore to establish an exact starting line. This station also contains a videotape camera that can record the starting line wire, the bows of all boats, and the starter's flag all in one view. The starter is located in a tower about 30 to 50 meters behind the starting line in the center of the course for clear viewing of the red flag, close enough to hear the starting commands through a loudspeaker system. Rowers are always told to start at the first movement of the flag as opposed to the directives of the announcer. At the NCAA finals, an electronic timer system is used to start all the clocks for all lanes simultaneously when the flag is lowered. Usually there is a target at the end of the race centered in each lane to help the cox position the boat down the racecourse.

The start of a six-shell sprint is one of the most tension-filled events that I have witnessed in sports. With aligned boats and rowers wound up as tight as clock springs, you can cut the tension with a knife as the teams are called to attention and the flag is raised overhead. You can almost hear the gurgling of stomachs churning as they anticipate the call to "Go!" with a quick downward movement of the flag. In one of our boats, the anxiety was so high at the start that one of our rowers would regurgitate over the side before the race began. To graduate from the Novice Crew Dad status, the witness of a start at a major regatta is a must.

The Course
Quality sprint courses are set up using the Albano buoy system. As a Novice Crew Dad, you can impress your coach and fellow parents with the knowledge of this 1/8" stainless steel wire grid system using suspended, small buoys 15 meters apart and running the length of the course. It is called the Albano system because the matrix of buoys originated at a rowing course in Albano, Italy. At Michigan State, we were blessed with a super assistant coach and course set-up man, Matt Weise. Matt represents the dedication of unseen work as illustrated by the new Michigan State University course at Lake Ovid near East Lansing, Michigan. Through his hard work, a competitive course was layed out and maintained to host the Big Ten Championship in 2002, just the third year after its inauguration.

With the above system, the buoys are placed on seven cables (six lanes), 4 feet below the water surface. They are anchored on each end and stabilized by lateral cables and anchors every 500 meters. The proper alignment of the buoys is part of the scenery and function of the racecourse. The course buoys begin with red, change to white, and then back to red at the end. With colors and distance markers, the cox knows where her team is at all times during the race to carry out the coach's strategy. In the "heat of the race," the cox can also feel the competitive boats around her and judge by the markers the amount of energy spent by the team and the amount left to complete a given distance. Along the course, stations are also positioned every 500 meters to determine and record intermediate times as well as the order of the boats. The times and positions of the boats are communicated to the judges' stand. Courses that are marked in perfect "military symmetry," the buoys aligned across the course from the side and diagonally, are in harmony with the discipline and preciseness of the sport of crew.

The Sprint Finish

The end of the course is marked by the judges' stand and is equipped like the alignment station with a vertical wire positioned with an opposing fixed object to establish the finish line. A camera is a crucial component of the judges' stand to capture the photofinishes. Many times a team relies on a photo at the end to find out the winner of a particular event, especially when three or four out of six boats come down to the "wire."

At the finish line, as the bow of the boat crosses, the flag is lowered and the order number is called out and recorded. In addition, a horn sounds signaling to the crew when they cross the finish line. At the NCAA Championships, a judge is assigned to each lane and presses a computer activated button as soon as the boat in the lane crosses the finish line. The time is recorded into the computer. Often, it is difficult to tell who won in a close race, given the angles and view-distortion created by the water and its surroundings. In some courses, a perforated air hose is stretched under the water at the finish. This bubble line is used to send up air bubbles, breaking the water's surface and allowing a better view of the bow balls of the shells crossing the finish line. In all cases, a video camera is used to ensure complete accuracy of the finish. It is at the stand where the judges calculate the times for each boat in every heat.

Courses are specified to have at least 100 meters beyond the finish line to come safely to a stop. There are several quality courses where the finish area is very tight. One cramped finish was at the Windermere Classic in Redwood Shores, California. As soon as the boats crossed the finish line, the cox had to give an immediate "check all" command. All eight rowers squared their oarblades into the water, and with their finish speed, the back water was flying.

The finish line is the most exciting if positioned where all can see the instant race results. It is where most Novice Crew Dad's huddle to witness the outcome.

The Launch

The launch docks are extremely important real estate at a regatta. Class A courses provide wooden docks to provide for the launching of at least three V8+ boats at the same time. This area has a lot of action, especially at large regattas with both the coming and going of crews, shells, and oars almost continuously. The Novice Crew Dad should be active here to give full support to his daughter at the beginning and ending of each race. The launch is where full teams yell for each of their boats, sing their fight songs, and cheer each crew team for a successful race at the beginning or a victory celebration at the end. It is at this spot where close-up pictures are taken to capture the excitement and game-face of each woman athlete and her coach. The Novice Crew Dad should be present at each launch and return, win or lose, because every rowing daughter gives everything she has regardless of the outcome!

8.2   Launch at Princeton Boathouse

All good race courses provide support facilities to make the race go smoothly and safely. The starting area supplies a simple repair station to provide minor adjustments to the equipment to help all teams. A spare oar may be required by the organizing committee to be stored in this area by each team. Also, a checkpoint is provided at major competition events like conference and regional championships to weigh each boat before racing. The V8+ boat must weigh at least 93 kg (205.03 lbs.) not including oars or detachable electronic speaker system. The V4+ must weigh at lease 51 kg (112.44 lbs.).

First-aid provisions are also required at each racecourse to attend to minor injuries and allow for emergency assistance calls. If emergency assistance is not available within ten minutes, an ambulance or paramedic unit is located at the course site.

To get the full flavor of the sport of crew, you, as the Novice Crew Dad, must experience the entire course from start to finish. Only then can you completely appreciate all elements of the race, even the ones that most spectators never see.

Course Lane and Positioning

Most sprint races are a two-out-of-three progressive system. Two heats are run to establish petite and grand finalists. Normally the first heats are run in the morning and create the semi-final round for the afternoon. Out of the semi-finals come the petite and grand (medal round) finalists. In a competitive sprint regatta on a Class A course, racing in the heats also establishes lane positions. Because of the wide variation in course conditions, the lane positions can be critical even on an "A" certified course. Lanes in the first heat are often provided by the way teams are ranked or seeded going into a regatta. The higher ranked teams are the higher seeded teams and given the middle preferred lanes to start. Once the first heat is run, a draw is made one time to determine the lanes assigned by heat and position. In a 6-lane race, the assignments are as follows:

Place	Lanes*+
1st and 2nd	3 and 4
3rd and 4th	2 and 5
5th and 6th	1 and 6
*Lanes for each pair are randomly drawn	
+With multiple heats, a draw is made to determine lanes, based on position in a heat.	

As previously mentioned, even a slight current in the middle of the course can add some advantage to a team. More importantly, the middle lanes provide a field advantage. Boats positioned in lanes 3 or 4 have full field view of the course and all the boats running. This allows the middle lane boats to know exactly where they are at all times in the race relative to the competitors, and have the distinct advantage of depth of full view to carry out or adjust their strategy.

Ranked 11th in the nation going into the 2003 South/Central Championships in Oak Ridge, Tennessee, the M.S.U. 1V8+ had expectations of a high place finish. After rowing in 3rd place in one of two semi-finals, the 1V8+ qualified for the outer lanes and was positioned in lane number 1 for the grand finals. As I rode my bike along the course to watch the race, it just seemed like the team was rowing "up hill" in lane number 1, closest to the bike path. The other teams appeared to have better water conditions. Whether it just wasn't "our day" or lane number 1 was just slow, we ended up in an unexpected 6th place. I believe that lane assignment does make a difference, real and psychological. Fighting for lane numbers 3 or 4 in the early heats can definitely make a difference in the final outcome. This is based on potentially better water conditions and a clearer view of the entire race across all six lanes.

The three W's, weather, water and way, are the make-up of an individual course. Even though the distance is the same, how you get from start to finish varies widely to prove that every race has its course and along with it, both variety and excitement.

CHAPTER 9

All in Your Head

Some of the most intriguing courses are those rowed in head races. The head races held in the fall season are grand events often with hundreds of participants ranging in age from juniors (high school) to masters (senior citizens). Head races are also not confined to one type of rowing; both sweep rowing and sculling are done down the racecourse, adding to the event's diversity. I had the opportunity to attend many multi-event head races across the country, all of which were spectacular. Some, like the Head of the Ohio, are held in conjunction with supporting a wonderful charity. In the head race, the boats have a "running" start and are at full speed when crossing the start line. Boats are released in approximately 15-second intervals. The course involves steering around river bends and under bridge abutments to complete the 5 to 6 kilometer race. The head races are used by college coaches to improve techniques as well as keep the team in shape and motivated for the spring sprints. They tend to be more relaxed and considered the "practice season" of the sport. For the "ice teams" like Michigan State, it is valuable water time before the team goes indoors to train on the dreaded erg machines. Their next reprieve on the water occurs when the team goes south at the end of Christmas break. I always envied my daughter going to Cocoa Beach, Florida when we had eight feet of snow and 15°F temperatures in Cleveland, Ohio. She countered with, "It's warm, but we row our asses off in preparation for the spring sprints."

The head races are not named after the source or head of the river or lakes, but instead reference the "race inside the head." Granted, all race courses require a battle within a rower's head, regardless of racecourse length and competitive environment. However, head races involve a few characteristics that make the event especially mentally challenging. First of all, these female rowers have been doing 6K erg tests for the previous two months. Their bodies and minds have been training to push out those evil voices saying nasty things like, "You have rowed for ten minutes and you are not even halfway done," or "Your legs are not going to be able to push off another 300 times (or another 3,000 meters)." Preparation for head races involves meeting these evil voices "head-on" and learning to counter-respond to them. Also, head races usually leave a shell racing against the clock, alone in the water. The coxswain and rowers must pull with the thought that each stroke matters, even if no boats are physically next to them. Lastly, the finish line is miles away.

Unlike sprints where the coxswain can announce, "I see the finish line," when in the third 500 meters, the head races rarely use this announcement at all. It is very common for the cox to not say anything about things outside of the shell. Again, this goes back to the internal nature of these races. All in all, head races differ greatly from the sprint season, ultimately making it a unique and special time. Rowers can attest that once those evil voices are told to "shut up," it can be one of the most empowering experiences throughout the rowing season.

The head races serve as great fun for the Novice Crew Dad, as well as an opportunity to study the sport. At these races, the coaches are relaxed, the rowers are relaxed, and there is not the pressure of the "head-to-head" competition and the NCAA rankings that go with the spring sprint season. These races are like the time trials at NASCAR where the mechanics are tuning up their cars, the drivers are getting a feel of the track, and all the teams are joking around, enjoying the sport without the pressure of race day.

CHAPTER 9 ALL IN YOUR HEAD

I learned more about the intricacies of the crew at these races when I could talk to the coaches and get to know the team members in a more informal setting. In NASCAR and women's crew, when the racing begins, the adrenaline flows, and game faces become serious as the competitive spirit bubbles up in every member connected with the team. The large head regattas create both joy and excitement with the pageantry of many boats, schools, and clubs, all with enthusiasm for the sport and a zest for competition. For midwesterners, the beautiful turning of the leaves into deep golds and reds only serves to heighten the special experience.

The following description of some of the head races around the country, along with some pictures, creates some visuals to entice you to attend the fall season head races. Although there is not the "head-to-head" competition, the display of many boat classifications, schools, and clubs creates a high energy atmosphere. It is also a time to watch your daughter compete and enough "down time" to stroll the grounds with her as she persuades you to buy her a T-shirt or other apparel. This is a time you don't want to miss in your journey as a Novice Crew Dad.

Head of the Ohio

The Head of the Ohio takes place in downtown Pittsburgh where the three rivers, the Ohio, the Allegheny, and the Monongahela meet. The finish line is located near Heinz Field, home of the Pittsburgh Steelers. The event is a great fundraiser organized by the Pittsburgh Mercy Health System and Three Rivers Rowing Club, raising money for the burn center. The logistics are excellent with launch and finish at the same spot and a great venue of ten bridges.

9.1 Head of the Ohio - Pittsburgh, Pennsylvania

Head of the Schuylkill

9.2 Head of the Schuykill
Philadelphia, PA

The Head of the Schuylkill is another premier fall Regatta in Philadelphia organized and hosted by the University Barge Club of Philadelphia. The regatta is boasted to be the world's largest one-day rowing event involving approximately 1,000 boats and 5,000 rowers. Including competitors from recreational, high school to college, masters, and veteran rowers, the race starts above the Strawberry Mansion Bridge and ends at the famous Boathouse Row, a spectacular row of boathouses, which are colorfully lit at night.

Head of the Lake

One of the most picturesque Head Races is the Head of the Lake beginning on Lake Union and finishing on Lake Washington in Seattle, Washington. The West Coast universities and others compete annually in the event organized by the Lake Washington Rowing Club, which was founded nearly 50 years ago to prepare talented rowers for the 1956 Olympics. This fall Classic is viewed from Montlake Boulevard Bridge overlooking the Lake Washington Ship Canal, between Lake Union and Lake Washington. The golden, fall colors of the poplar trees, mixed with the northwest pines, make this regatta a must for any Novice Crew Dad. I was

9.3　　　Head of the Lake
View from Montlake Boulevard Bridge

proud of myself for flying from Cleveland, Ohio to attend this event, and boasted that I was the biggest fan of my daughter's team, only to later learn that other parents drove three days straight from Michigan just to watch their daughter row. Biggest fan, move over.

Lake Washington Rowing Club invited all the teams and parents to a lasagna dinner at the LWRC boathouse the night before the race. The Rowing Club displayed some of the best hospitality and friendliness in my four years of Head Racing regattas. The University of Washington, a frequent NCAA Women's Collegiate Champion (1997, 1998, 2001), has a great tradition of quality female rowers, along with great coaches. Viewing Lake Washington, I understood why the teams were so good. The brisk weather and choppiness of Lake Washington makes for the "perfect storm" while practicing. When the teams from U. of W. row in smooth conditions, they probably think they hit the heavenly waters, and begin to row at warp speed.

While in Seattle, our team visited the Pocock Racing Shells, founded in that area in 1911. The company is an innovator in carbon fiber/kevlar construction (their Hypocarbon™ series), and have supplied shells to crews at many universities. The team enjoyed viewing the design and construction of the shells, especially since they spend twenty hours a week with their butts "glued" to their seats.

Head of the Charles

Perhaps the most famous head race in the United States is the Head of the Charles. It began in 1965 and has grown to be not only the signature event of the Charles River every autumn, but also one of the largest regattas in the country. Situated just south of prestigious Harvard University, the Head of the Charles radiates with collegiate rowing tradition. This event, however, is not reserved for just male and female college athletes. The regatta spans every age group and skill level within the sport of rowing. It is the Mecca, if you will, of rowing within the United States. Standing on one of the many bridges towering above, the boats look more like vehicles in the morning rush hour commute than peaceful, gliding shells. Here, more than ever, the coxswains' directional skill is tested. It is the Head of the Charles where many major women's collegiate rowing programs in the nation battle against each other to "show their stuff," debuting exciting things to come.

Princeton Chase

The Princeton Chase is a three-mile invitational head race hosted by the Princeton University crew coaching staff. The race is actually 2-3/4 miles on Lake Carnegie, with spectacular views from Harrison Street Bridge or the finish at the Washington Road Bridge, located near Princeton's beautiful and historic boathouse. Normally comprised of the eastern and Ivy League schools, it is a colorful and exciting event for both men's and women's crews as the boats make the turn and come straight at the finish line, just short of the Washington Road Bridge.

9.4　　　　　Princeton Chase
View from Washington Road Bridge

Other Head Races

There are many other head races held throughout the country; most of them are held in the months of September and October. These races define the sport of crew, which is about teamwork and the opportunities to test the very physical and mental limits of the inner self. Although there are medals that come with Head races, they are a distant second to achieving a team best or a personal record.

For the Novice Crew Dads, there are plenty of sites to see at these head regattas. Topped with a day outing of picnic lunches and great camaraderie with the teams, parents, and coaches, these are events you want to make a family gathering. Going to the heads is a very "heady" time for all!

CHAPTER 10

Sprint to the Finish

The Sprints

The sprints are the races that exude the competitive spirit of collegiate rowing. Women's rowing is especially exciting based on a higher variability in emotions that can lead to unpredictable results and outcomes. Women rowers have excellent techniques, and, as in many other women's sports, there is always the hair and look (sunglasses and hats) that are important.

Held in the spring, these races are side-by-side, head-to-head, oar-to-oar in a 2,000-meter course, lasting from approximately 6.6 to 7.2 minutes for a women's eight, all dependent on course, lane position, and weather conditions. The race starts from a dead stop staked (held at a dock) or floating (sometimes from a rope across the starting area) and can involve two (dual meet) to 6 (even 7) shells in a large regatta. A 6.6-minute winning time represents a boat speed of approximately 11.3 miles per hour (18.2 kilometers per hour), in a lane 44 feet wide charted out with buoyed marked lanes on a river, lake, or reservoir.

The sprints are the culmination of a year's worth of summer workouts, fall head races, winter erging and weight training, and spring tune-up for each crew team to "give it all they've got!" The spring competition is the most exciting for the spectators, and heart throbbing for the Novice Crew Dad, seeing your daughter and her teammates pulling with every ounce of energy in one complete synchronous motion.

These regattas, held from March through June, resemble an Olympic experience with only a few chances (usually double elimination) to do well after seven months of grueling conditioning and training.

Sprints are won and lost by tenths or hundredths of a second and truly represent the thrill of victory and agony of defeat in one event. Emotional highs and lows come at all levels for parents, student athletes, coaches, and everyone connected to the sport.

One of my first emotional lows was at the Big Ten Championship held at Belleville Lake with host University of Michigan. My daughter, Kirsten, rowed in the Second Varsity Eight in the qualifying heat for the Grand Final, the medal round. As the boats passed us near the U. of M. boathouse, they were in a real dogfight with Wisconsin for second place (the top two teams of the heat went to the Grand). The finish line was "down the lake" and we could not see who won. The announcer calling the race blurted out, "It's a photo finish between Michigan State and Wisconsin for second place." As a Novice Crew Dad, you wait in agony for the results. When the announcer gave the times: **Michigan State 6:34.50 - Wisconsin 6:34:28**, it proved that Wisconsin won by 22 one-hundredths of a second; my heart sank to my stomach. Covering 1.25 miles in a little over six and one-half minutes means M.S.U. lost by approximately 3 feet. That's heartbreaking!

In rowing, win or lose, each team rows back to the launch and carries the shell back to the team's landing.

When I got back to the team's tent, all the women were crying, and there was just nothing, as a crew Dad, you could think to say. This was an agonizing moment, but one that exemplifies the sport's ability to prepare you well for life's challenges.

Having followed the Michigan State Crew Team over the four years of my daughter's involvement, I had the opportunity to witness many sprint regattas. These were great events and fun times to watch competition at its best - win or lose.

CHAPTER 10 SPRINT TO THE FINISH

From a Rower's Perspective

10.1 Win or Lose
The boat is carried back

The sport of rowing is really for the participants and not for the spectators. The dedication and commitment for a woman athlete to rise up at 5:00 a.m. and exert her body to full exhaustion is considered a "mystery of the crew cranium." Many of my daughter's fellow rowers have expressed the magnificent beauty of an early morning sunrise, the majestic serenity of mist rising about the still water, and the "rush" feeling of complete harmony as the sound of each oar sings in unison with seven other rowers. This full exertion of mind, body, and spirit, all combined with the competitive human element, creates the passion for the Sprints.

Have Shell, Will Travel

The Spring season usually starts with dual meets or small regattas where three or four schools compete. Once each practice week is over and seat racing completed, the coaches determine the line-ups for each boat. The team is then ready to race at their home course or become the visitor at an away regatta. To compete away, travel is usually set via a large team bus that can accommodate sixty women. Bus time is a real team-building experience with plenty of chances to bond with fellow teammates. Our team was blessed with John Ricci, a resident driver who took care of all the driving and became an integral part of the M.S.U. rowing community, encouraging the women and partnering with all the parents.

Usually the shells are transported separately with a truck and trailer rig and driven by members of the team staff. When the journey is across the country, the core team, consisting of the 1V8+ and 2V8+, and the 1V4+ fly commercial aircraft, sometimes taking along the oars. Normally a shell is borrowed from the hosting university. I remember the Head of the Lake in Seattle, Washington, when Michigan State borrowed both a boat and oars from Stanford. It was a bit odd locating our team on the water, decked out in our green and white race uniforms, sporting the cardinal color oars. Rowing past the tall pines in the northwest, we looked like Santa's sleigh on water.

Game Day

On game day, preparations start early. Feeding sixty women with high metabolisms is the first task and usually starts with high carb bagels. A run to the local bagel shop or bakery is a very convenient way to feed "en masse," although I always questioned if bagels were a victory diet. Certainly, with all the energy about to be spent, a trip to the carbohydrate bank was probably the right deposit. The breakfast for sixty famished women always reminds me of our family reunions where eating is a competitive event.

After the quick-carb feast, the rowers' minds shift to the real competition that's about to take place. The team loads the bus, and silence takes over as each woman rower begins to visualize the course and the stroke sequence that is about to take place. Visualization is common among slalom skiers who plan in their head every turn they will take in a downhill course. Rowers use the same "mind's eye" to harmonize their body with the shell and the course.

When the bus arrives at the site and the team disembarks, there are three things that every crew member goes through. The first is the deploying and rigging of the boats while making final mechanical adjustments for course and strategy. Secondly, all women begin stretching and limbering movements to work out any kinks and prepare the anatomy for complete taxation. Finally, the third movement is the 40-yard dash to the outhouse.

In high profile regattas like the Big Ten Conference and NCAA Championships, drug testing is administered. These tests are administered randomly to teams and currently involve a urine sample. Soon, the NCAA will be able to use the hair follicle test, which is very stringent because enhancement drugs can be stored for many months in these glands and are readily detected. The NCAA follows the definition of stimulants based on the anti-doping rules of the US Olympic Committee, as well as the bylaws of FISA, the International Rowing Standards Association.

While the activity of the rowers is taking place, the coach submits the team lineup by boats. According to the rules, substitutions can be made up to half of the rowers, including the cox, but it must be done in writing at least one hour before the first race. After the first race, no substitutions are allowed in a boat, except for illness.

This is a time, also, when the weight of the boat and coxswain are measured to ensure parity in equipment and dead weight. The boats are weighed with large scales and chosen at random in the key events like Big Ten and NCAA Championships. Most other races for Big Ten teams are on the honor system. As mentioned previously, the weight of an eight shell must be a minimum of 205.03 lbs. (93 kg). A four-man shell must be at least 112.44 lbs. (51 kg). Shells are weighed also after racing and are subject to scrutiny at any time.

Besides the boat, the coxswain is also weighed once per day, one to two hours before the scheduled time of the first race. Weighing of these crew "quarterbacks" is done in full uniform without any footwear, tools, or electronic devices. The cox must weigh a full 110 lbs. or must add a ballast adjustment if she is less than the minimum. With the weight of the boat and cox established, the cox and the "eight-seats" return to camp to huddle with the coach.

Coach's Corner

Unlike most sports, crew does not permit coaching during the race. When I asked Coach Bebe Bryans about the inability to coach during the race, she responded: "It makes you want to vomit." Having coached both my daughters in basketball, I could not imagine sitting on the bench and not being able to say a word to the team for the whole game! As Bebe explained, the best antecedent is not Maalox® (brand name of the Novartis Company), but "complete confidence in the young women and their abilities to race." "In rowing," according to Coach Bryans, "the goal of a coach is to be unnecessary during race day." The coach is unnecessary because the strategy is set before any racing takes place. The plan is geared specifically to maximize the strength of the team. Some teams start fast, others are better finishers. The coach sets the plan to optimize speed. The only time the coach may alter a best-known strategy for a particular boat is when the coach knows that the team will be outclassed. This is the time when an uncommon race plan may be used to try to break a competitor's momentum. The obvious objective for any coach is to win as many races as possible.

The race plan is communicated by the coach to the coxswain. The better the coxswain's abilities to multi-task (i.e., steer the boat, know the stroke count, know the position of the boat in the race, and know the fatigue signs of each rower), the more the cox can call her own race.

The cox needs the ability and race moxie, just like a football quarterback reads defenses and calls "audibles" at the line of scrimmage. The crew coach sets the race plan, but the better coxswains can read the race and make adjustments to win. The cox must know her teammates and when to make a move, just like a jockey must know the horse and position it for victory.

With the race plan set, the coach's primary mission immediately before a race is to be the cheerleader, instilling the confidence of the entire team and rousing the will to win. As the crew breaks from the huddle, emotionally charged, the cox takes control with comments to carry the shell to the launch dock. Once the shell is in the water, the oars set, and last minute personal adjustments made, the coach often will attend to each rower. I always admired the personal

10.2 Coach's "Right to Remain Silent"

touch of Coach Bebe, who would give one last verbal confidence booster done with a physical hug to each racer. Without the ability to coach from that moment, this personal touch is a key success ingredient to drive human emotion. The coach then takes a key viewing position on the course or peddles a bike to the start to witness in "silence."

Off to the Races
Once the women are positioned in their seats and begin to push off, the rest of the members of the most spirited teams break into a rousing chorus of the school fight song. At this launch moment, the enthusiasm and togetherness of a team can be measured by the decibel level achieved as they cheer their team to victory. With the launch completed, the coach goes into the thought bank and begins the "right to remain silent" as the team rows to the starting position. As a rower, hearing and seeing your other teammates, coaches, and fans scream the fight song as you push away from land, the emotion cannot be adequately expressed. It is like your spirit coming alive, and you are reminded just how lucky you are to be doing this.

Racing - A Daughter's View (Inside the Shell)
Usually the launch dock is near the finish of the race, so the teams must row the course distance to the start. This is the last time to get mentally prepared for what is to come. At this time, each rower will breathe easy and push away any worries that may clutter the mind. It is a last minute tune-up for technique to maximize the fundamentals of every stroke. Sometimes, there is even a stop to cheer on another team boat as they pass on the course. Reaching the starting tower, the team positions the boat into the assigned lane.

The Start
Most starts are done with a stake or a person holding the stern of the boat to ensure alignment. The cox and bow seat make sure that the boat is properly aligned for a true start.

If not ready, the bow seat signals by raising her hand conspicuously in the air. The coxswain will usually ask bow or two seat to take a stroke or to back it up. With currents and weather factors, this can go on for what seems like an eternity. The starter polls the boats, calling each boat by name for readiness. "Attention" is called and a red flag is raised. The starter will call "Go" with a quick downward motion of the red flag. The crews may start when the red flag begins

10.3 Stake Start - Columbus, Ohio

to move. If the bow of the boat crosses the start line before the starter's flag begins to move, it constitutes a false start. If a team creates two false starts, their boat will be removed from the race.

When conditions are windy and the teams have trouble aligning, normal starting procedures will change to "countdown start." The starter will use a cadence of 5, 4, 3, 2, 1, "Attention!" "Go!," and it is up to each crew to align the boat themselves to get the best start possible.

With Olympic rowing, a cradle device, also referred to as a "boot," locks each boat into position and ensures both alignment and no chance for a false start. At the "Go!" command, the boot holding each boat simultaneously drops below the hulls, creating an absolute even start. There are only a few of these systems available and are reserved for the Olympic regattas to create the fairness demanded of this high profile world event.

Inside the Mind of a Stroke

There is a big difference between the Novice Crew Dad's view of the race and the race that goes on from a rower's perspective. In order to acquire a feel of a sprint race, I interviewed Krista Buzzell, an all-American, who stroked the Michigan State team 1V8+ in both 2001 and 2002. The following comments are paraphrased from Krista's interview, start to finish: "A rower should always be mentally focused on the race in the same way, but thoughts vary from race to race depending on the competition, the weather, and how the individual feels physically at that moment."

Start

As the team is sitting coiled like a snake ready to strike at the start, Krista's heart and mind are already racing. *Once I get to pull the first stroke, it's all gonna come together. Watch the flag, relax, relax, you're ready, you can do this, just like practice, easier than practice, watch the flag, relax, feeling confident. It's not just me, seven other super-strong people, training there for me to go hard the whole way, kicking ass, and fighting like bulldogs. Then, I realize I'm thinking too much and just need to bring all those thoughts in, slow my heart down, and think about all of that energy being right in my quads and ready to fire when that flag drops. In the last seconds before that flag drops, I focus my mind to only think about pushing with my heels as soon as I see the flag drop and pretend nothing else is going on around me.*

10.4 The start: flag drops, push with everything you've got

500-Meter Mark

Thoughts here also vary. Wow, that was a fast first 500, or it's about time. Thinking about how the boat is feeling, how I'm feeling, what I could be doing better. Focus on the call the coxswain just made or trying not to think about anything and letting my mind find a zone that detaches me from the gradual burn that is building.

1,000-Meter Mark
Okay, half way, best part is yet to come as I love the gradual build to the sprint. Time to focus on technique, only pulling harder: Don't give into taking one "off" stroke.

1,500-Meter Mark
Home stretch, just get through the next 300 and it's twenty strokes from there. Feelin' good, feelin' strong, focus, focus.

Last 200 Meters
Okay, these last twenty strokes are not so easy: I swear we should be done; pull harder, pull faster, drop the blade in and jump, get this over with!

From inside the shell, the mind, the body, and the spirit all cross the finish line when the flag is lowered; the last boat number is called and the horn sounds signaling the end to the crew. As learned from Krista's commentary, the race from inside the shell is a totally different experience than the Novice Crew Dad's view from shore, although sometimes both daughter and Dad end with total exhaustion.

With the race completed, the boat comes to a complete stop while the rowers gather themselves, both physically and mentally. Usually, at this point, the infamous slump of the body is seen where the entire anatomy folds into exhaustion. As all the seat rowers collect themselves, they begin their return to the launch dock. As the crew returns, they are normally met by the coach and other teammates to celebrate or comfort, and help them with the gear. This is another crucial moment for the Novice Crew Dad to be present, as your daughter just left "everything" she had on the water. This is the time when that father-daughter relationship is brought to new heights. No matter the outcome, you know she was a fierce competitor. Win, lose, or draw, the crew lifts the 200-pound shell from the water to the shoulder and carries the boat back to camp. After a few moments pause, the crew gathers around the coach to analyze the race.

Often the coach will have the digital information from the Speed Coach™ (trademark of Nielsen-Kellerman), an onboard "computer." The digital information is obtained from this electronic device on the bottom of the hull that records times every 100 meters to analyze the entire distance. The coach's words are chosen carefully to match the expectations of all versus the actual outcome.

It is after the team breaks the huddle that your daughter is approachable. This is where I recommend a big hug from Dad, no matter the race result. Sometimes, I would act as a surrogate hugger for other team members. I had a special hug connection with Jackie Boswell, who was a good friend of my daughter's and a hugger extraordinaire. Besides a physical hug, I found that the best words were in the form of a question, "How did it feel out there?" Regardless of the answer, another hug follows, all in the "name of the father and daughter."

Racing - A Dad's View (A View From Shore)

Rowing, from the eyes of the Novice Crew Dad on shore, is a very different experience than from the eyes of the daughter in the sliding seat.

Planning and Preparation

The planning and preparation of the Novice Crew Dad, although not as physically demanding as the team's preparation, are very similar. The first step is to get the sprint schedule early in the spring season and plan the trips to maximize your support. Planning involves trips by car, and sometimes by plane, and requires increasing preparation, especially if you are a parental team captain (*Battle of the Parents*, CHAPTER 11,).

It is important that you allow plenty of travel time in order to make the team's, and at the very minimum, your daughter's first race. In a two-day sprint regatta, your daughter will usually race only three times for a total of about twenty minutes, so your timing is extremely critical. When we lived in Toronto, Ontario, I would often tell my daughter, that as parents, we would drive an hour for every minute she rowed. As good parents and a proud Novice Crew Dad, I would do it anyway. The facts are, the amount of time your daughter trains, practices, and competes far outweighs the parent time invested. I remember one South/Central race in Oak Ridge, Tennessee, where parents of a crewmate got lost and arrived after their daughter finished first in their heat, coming from behind to win. After the race, when asked of the parents, "Did you see it? Did you see it?," the only answer was "Great race, sweetheart." With so little race time, my advice is go early and stay late to take advantage of the unique experience.

Once you have decided to get to the race on time, dress is the next most important. The novice races are always the first off and usually begin around 8:00 a.m. In those early spring mornings in April, I learned that crew was not necessarily a warm weather sport, especially in Big Ten country. Even the crew teams had to use their pogies, or hand warmers, over the oar handles on those frosty mornings. Dress must include sweatshirts with hood, windbreakers, and hats (baseball or stocking). Of course, our all-weather gear must be in school colors to win the "Battle of the Parents." Pack your rain gear, sunglasses, and sunscreen because you need all of it to survive the weekend. Another dress essential are "duck shoes" or waterproof boots, as most crewing events are soggy, especially when you view the launch, which is a must for full Dad support.

A Clear View

For complete viewing and recording of the event, a camera with a telephoto lens and binoculars are absolutely necessary. The sport of crew is a natural for some of the best sport pictures that you can shoot with the scenery, the colors and, of course, the athletes. The best pictures come from being in a launch boat or the official's boat as the race progresses. The pictures of synchronized sweeping and the vivid facial expressions are absolutely priceless. The next best thing is the telephoto lens from a bridge or bank to get the full frontal view. I started shooting pictures with a Nikon N80 single reflex camera using a 70-210 mm lens and quickly upgraded to a 70-300 mm lens for closer capability. Many times, I wished I had gone for a 100-400 mm or even a professional's longer lens to really capture the women on the water. Without a tripod, I used ASA 800-speed film to compensate for the jiggling of the camera. In any event, a first class 35 mm or digital camera with a telescopic lens is a must to capture the event, or in particular, a moment of glory for your daughter and her team. In addition, the crew friends' shots are the most memorable, as there is plenty of non-racing time to capture the fun, spirit, and camaraderie of the sport.

Binoculars are the second essential item so that you can "pick up" the start (view the flag), and most importantly, view as much of the race as possible. Standing at the finish line, with small sport binoculars, 7x20, you can view the race at the 1,000-meter mark. Even without knowing the lane position, it is possible to spot the oar blade design and colors in order to follow the team. As a Novice Crew Dad, I was able to see the evenness of strokes, synchronization, clean catches (minus splash), and effort to move the boat through the water. It is still difficult to see who is leading with the angles and parallax that normally exists in watching. I was always amazed at coaches who could tell from 1,000 meters, through binoculars, the exact position of their team. Binoculars are a must to get in more viewing time per race.

Sprints Around the U.S.A.

My connection to Michigan State led me to most sprints held in the Big Ten country of the Midwest, known as the Central Region. I was very fortunate to also attend sprints held in the east, south, and west regions, which were equally exciting. Some, like at Stanford and Princeton, were steeped with a long and rich tradition of crew. Although there are hundreds of great sprint races held across the U.S., I have chosen to describe four regattas that capture the flavor and spirit of NCAA 2000-meter venues.

Princeton Open Crew - The East

There is nothing like the tradition of eastern schools when it comes to crew, especially the rich tradition of the Ivy League. Men's rowing began its heritage in the East, influenced by the early British connection to the Henley-on-the-Thames-River. With early history imbedded in New England culture, it was only natural that women's rowing would blossom from crew's "flowerbed" of the East Coast.

The Princeton Open Crew Sprint is held on Carnegie Lake in Princeton, New Jersey, and is raced in the opposite direction from the Fall Classic head race, the Princeton Chase. This race has traditionally been a cup race between Princeton and Brown Universities, and recently Big Ten teams were invited to participate. The entire surrounding of the campus, the boathouse, and the immaculate facilities, all embody the ambiance of rowing.

Just one walk through the Princeton boathouse and you understand why this place is special. The history, the legendary pictures, the décor, and the neatness all radiate the energy of a rowing capital. As I witnessed the event, and realized our Midwest daughters were competing with the women from Princeton and Brown, I knew we were in a place of honor. With the quality of the communication about the race, the exactness of times, the precision of the launch, and the crispness of the announcing, you could feel the professionalism of the Princeton Open Regatta.

This eastern school and eastern event at Princeton, New Jersey creates a certain excitement that should not be missed by the Novice Crew Dad.

Windermere Collegiate Crew Classic - The West

Right behind the rich eastern universities' rowing tradition is the western waterscape. The western schools are led

CHAPTER 10 SPRINT TO THE FINISH 101

10.5 The Windermere Classic
Windermere Shores, California

by the University of Washington women's program, formed in the early 70's. The Windermere Collegiate Classic is held at the Redwood Shores in Redwood City, California, located just south of the city of San Francisco. I labeled this event as "country club rowing at its best." Perfect weather combined with perfect water (not even a ripple), and perfect host, Stanford University, all combine to generate the club label. The Bay Area beauty and majestic viewing make the regatta a must on the curriculum to graduate from the Novice Crew Dad status. Being at the Redwood Shores for crew is equivalent to floor seats at a NBA game, the best view in professional sports.

10.6 Rope Start
Redwood Shores, California

South/Central Championships - Oak Ridge Tennessee

Teams from the Big Ten, along with the other central region participants, are late-comers to the rowing "party" compared to the East and West Coast teams. The "ice schools," as well as those schools south of the Mason-Dixon Line and inward, compete for the South/Central Region Championships. Even though most of these schools are in a steep learning curve, the competitiveness increases exponentially each year and will eventually give the coast schools a run for the NCAA Championship. The northern schools are somewhat hindered by water practice time, but it is my belief that they will find a way to compete and win by sheer will and determination.

The South/Central Championships are held every year at Lake Melton in Oak Ridge, Tennessee. This course is the best for active Novice Crew Dads with roller blades or a bicycle.

The Oak Ridge course contains the active Dad's three P's: park, pedal, and picnic. At Lake Melton, it is easy to park the car next to the course, unload your bike to pedal the full length of the lake, and use the grounds for a team picnic. This site is one that the active Novice Crew Dad can appreciate.

Host, University of Tennessee, with co-host and sponsor, Lexus, offers Southern hospitality to each participating school. Protected by pine trees and nestled in a

10.7   Coaches', Spectators' bike path

valley just north of the Smokey Mountains, this event offers both a beautiful setting and a classy affair for teams coming of age in women's crew.

The region of the South/Central universities is comprised of twenty-nine teams spread over twelve conferences located throughout the South, Southwest, and Midwest. All the Big Ten teams with women's varsity programs are represented at this Championship. The Big Ten Conference, plus teams from eleven other conferences make this one of the most colorful rowing spectacles. The conferences and schools who are currently attending are:

Atlantic Coast Conference	Clemson, Duke, North Carolina, and Virginia
Atlantic Sun Conference	Stetson, Jacksonville, Central Florida
Atlantic 10 Conference	Dayton
Big East Conference	Miami (FL), Notre Dame
Big Ten Conference	Indiana, Iowa, Michigan, Michigan State, Minnesota, Ohio State, Wisconsin
Big 12 Conference	Kansas, Kansas State, Texas
Conference USA	Cincinnati and Louisville
Ohio Valley Conference	Murray State
Mid-American Conference	Eastern Michigan
Missouri Valley Conference	Creighton, Drake
Southeast Conference	Tennessee
Western Athletic Conference	Southern Methodist, Tulsa

CHAPTER 10 SPRINT TO THE FINISH 103

The South/Central Championships play a big role in the bids for the NCAA Finals. The winner normally gets an automatic bid and is joined by other teams and 1V8+ boats that finish strong in Oak Ridge, while having solid performances at other spring sprints. These races represent one of the best settings for the Novice Crew Dad to really "get into" the sport.

NCAA Championships - Geographic Rotation

The culmination of spring sprint races is the NCAA Championships. When the top teams and top 1V8+ boats compete from all three divisions, it makes for a spectacular show. The Championship started in 1997, with locations rotating around the country from Sacramento, California in the West to Camden, New Jersey in the East, to Gainesville, Georgia in the South, and Indianapolis, Indiana in the Central. I was fortunate to attend two back-to-back championships at Eagle Creek in Indianapolis, Indiana. The site at Eagle Creek is excellent for viewing and is ideally set-up for the privacy of the teams and the interaction of the spectators.

To be invited to the NCAA Championships is a real honor and it is another must for any Crew Dad. Regardless of where the event is held, the NCAA's are the showcase of women's collegiate rowing. It is this regatta where a national champion is crowned, and based on many variables in crew, any team or individual boat has a chance to win.

10.8   NCAA Championships - Eagle Creek
        Indianapolis, Indiana

Look for the greatest enthusiasm and the ultimate competitiveness, as the pinnacle of "W" Crew is on stage for all to watch.

Sprint to the Finish

The sprints are what women's crew is all about -- each athlete, each boat, each team, reaching deep inside their physical and mental being to give it all they have. Rowers and coaches sprint to the finish of their season, focusing all energy on the NCAA Championships, with parents and fans supporting them the entire distance. From a global perspective, the sport of Women's U.S. Rowing is starting to become even more of an international presence. The energy surrounding the sprints has never been more intense. We have front row seats! One day, "Sprint to the Finish" will make a great and inspiring film!

CHAPTER 11

Battle of the Parents

In my opinion, the most colorful and exciting atmosphere of all sports is college football. Saturday afternoon in the Big Ten marks the battle of the athletes, the battle of the coaches, and the battle of the bands, all with tens of thousands of students, parents, fans, and alumni enjoying the pageantry.

Although there are not tens of thousands of people at a regatta, there are still great battles that go on. In crew, there is the battle of the athletes, the battle of the coaches, and the battle of the parents. The battle of the parents involves knowledge of the sport, the scoring of the event, closeness to the coaches, how you look, and most important, how you act. The battle of the parents is key because it's the parents of the rowers who are the cornerstone of the fans watching the race.

Preparation for Battle

Regattas, whether heads or sprints, are held all over the nation, and the best crew parents must plan and organize along with the crew teams to ensure the battle of the parents can be won.

The first step in preparation for parent battle is to coordinate and rally the parents of your team. My wife, Carol, and I showed up at the first regatta not knowing a soul. As in many sports, the varsity parents of seniors were huddled off in small groups, and there was not a lot of consolidation of parents. A strong cohesive group is needed for total parental victory. As the four years unfold, you get to know the other parents, whose daughter belongs to which parent, who belongs in what boat, and who sits on what seat of the boat (which is forever changing).

There is great solidarity in the parents of crew teams because of the amount of downtime spent together at a regatta (just like a swimming meet). The recommendation here is to take charge as a Novice Crew Dad (or Mom) and organize the parents early to prepare for the parental battle.

Rowing, unlike other sports, can be faceless with no names on the backs of uniforms. No names on football jerseys has become a recent college trend to put the emphasis back on team. For many years, only Joe Paterno, long-time football coach of Penn State, was the trendsetter with no names on football uniforms. I was happy to see newly-appointed Michigan State head football coach, John L. Smith, adopt this same philosophy. Other coaches are now following with this idea to counteract the "me generation" and truly state that there is no "I" in team.

In crew, with no names or numbers on the individual rowers, dads need help with identification. When I first started watching the races, I would mistake another rower for my own daughter! This was caused by my own inexperience, "over 50" set of eyes, and under-powered binoculars. Luckily, there is one break that parents get to view their daughter in the shell. According to the rules, individuals may wear headgear of their own choosing that does not have to be identical with other crew members. I saw everything from completely dyed hair, to bandannas, visors, hats, and sunglasses. I was able to quickly pick out my daughter by her headgear. It also gives each female a chance to make a personal statement. The statement, of course, must be approved by the coach!

Continuing with the theme of consolidation and unity, parent captains should be established. Just like in any team sport, captains are elected to get the signs from the coaches and then call the signals. Parent captains, usually self-elected, are the key personnel in the parental battles for

CHAPTER 11 BATTLE OF THE PARENTS 107

your women's crew team. I would recommend that every collegiate team have five parent captains: personnel, stakeout, dress, food, and scoring.

Personnel Captain

The Personnel Captain is the first captain who needs to be in place. Remembering the parents' names and the names of their daughters is especially challenging when you may see them, at most, five to ten times in a year. Personnel captains organize a list with all the parents' names and their daughters, including class status, e-mail addresses, home and mobile phone numbers.

Women, boats, and positions can change as often as the weather conditions in the Central Region. Once the names are secured of "who's on first," parent/daughter rosters can be helpful for the other captains and all the other parents.

Stakeout Captain

To win the parental battles at each race, a key captain must be nominated to stake out your team's position at the regatta. The Stakeout Captain usually is a person who can arrive a day early and claim the best piece of land to position a rallying and viewing spot for the other parents, their daughters, coaches, and alumni. This captain must have some gypsy in him or her or be familiar with the NASCAR life of moving from race to race. This captain is the one who owns or borrows a first-class tent with school colors and logos.

11.1   Staking the tent at NCAA Finals

A tent that matches the team's tent and is easy to put up is best for the stakeout. Along with the tent, a logo flag flying high for easy location by all is essential. A bonus is having several coordinated foldout logo chairs to place around the tent area.

Dress Captain (Parental Attire)

Once you have the names and places staked out, effort must be taken to coordinate the dress of the parents. To win the parental battle, not only do you need numbers of parents (strength in numbers), but all should be coordinated in the school colors. A jacket was sold to many parent boosters by the dress captain. The jacket looked neat and gave us a first class image, important in the battle of looks for in and out-of-conference regattas.

Food Captain (Captain "Crunch")

With all the people identified, their dress coordinated, and the stakeout completed, the most important person is the Food Captain. The Parental Food Captain has the most time consuming job of all five captains. The food is important because the women rowers are always starved, and the regatta usually has a lunch break between morning and afternoon sessions. Although many parents leave after the last race, some of our total parental victories came from the barbecues after the race was over, regardless of how the team fared.

Our Michigan State team was blessed with Food Tri-Captains. Three wonderful couples, the Hicks, the Penningtons, and the Yauks, would drive to every regatta with trucks, trailers and SUV's toting barbecue grills, roasters, and all the utensils, along with the gourmet food!

For the South/Central Championships in 2003, the couples drove to Oak Ridge, Tennessee with all the gear and put on a total team celebration after the races were over, and everyone else had gone home.

11.2   After South/Centrals - Team Celebration

CHAPTER 11 BATTLE OF THE PARENTS

The Michigan State team showed a united front and real bonding with the barbecue, including chicken, beef, corn-on-the-cob, pies, and cakes. Our gourmet cook on our team was Joette Yauk. Often she would bring wonderful and creative dishes to our crew races. She was famous for her "crew stew," which was enjoyed by all, especially on those cold, windy days. We enjoyed it so much, we wanted to share her recipe:

JOETTE'S CREW STEW
Smoked Turkey, Sweet Potato, and Corn Chowder

1 cup butter
8 tablespoons precooked bacon, can or pouch
2 large onions, diced
4 teaspoons fresh basil
2 teaspoons fresh thyme
1 cup flour
4 cups of whole kernel corn
2 red peppers, diced
2 lbs sweet potatoes, diced
2 cups water
12 cups chicken stock
4 lbs smoked turkey, cut into ½ inch cubes
3 cups milk
2 tablespoons salt
½ teaspoon black pepper

Melt butter and sauté bacon, onion, basil and thyme in a large soup pot until onion is soft, approximately 5 minutes. Add flour and mix well. Stir in corn, red pepper and sweet potatoes, sauté for 5 minutes. Add water, chicken stock and smoked turkey and bring to a boil. Stir in milk, salt and paper and return to a boil. Continue cooking until stew has thickened. Stir in chopped parsley or tarragon.

This recipe makes about a gallon of stew. You will have to up-size the recipe to accommodate the size of your crew, coaches, and fans!

The coaches are probably the most appreciative of the cookouts because their love of the sport is reinforced from the energy given back to not only the team, but also the parents who support the team!

Scoring Captain

Every team needs a parental captain of scoring. Not only is there no scoreboard in crew, the point system needs to be tabulated. It is weighted with the most points being awarded in the 1V8+ race, the finale of a sprint regatta. The scoring captain really becomes essential when your team is in the thick of the race for overall team competition. We had Peter Thomas, an engineer from the University of Illinois as our scoring captain. His talents were especially valuable at the Big Ten, the South/Central, and the NCAA Championships. With the graduated scale of points awarded, the race standings could change dramatically up until the very last race, the 1V8+.

11.3   M.S.U. 2V8+ Big Ten Champs 2003

Therefore, when the points are announced or posted during the race, it can be very misleading until the final race is finished. This is a true Yogi Berra sport - "It's never over until it's over." Because of the point system scale, the scoring captain can tell you exactly what has to happen and what places the teams must achieve to win the event. This makes it more interesting as the regatta comes to finality. Because many parents are in a haze, the parent scoring captain allows for greater interest through the entire event. Although every rower is a winner, champions are acknowledged with trophies and medals based on total points won.

CHAPTER 11 BATTLE OF THE PARENTS

Because the parents are the core fans, the core spectators, and, in essence, are the crowd, they substitute for the battle of the bands at a college football game. Like the bands at a football game, the parents represent the look, the voice, and the pageantry of the sport. Although no instrument is played, there is plenty of noise that comes from the parent section, including laughter, shouts, and endless cheering.

Early on, the battle of the parents is won on looks. Parents who show up in a rag-tag tent without logos and team color coordination can lose the first battle of perception of who they are and whom they represent. Personnel, Stakeout, and Dress Captains are crucial to winning those early perception battles at each regatta. As the race moves to late morning of the first day, the perception battle changes to the battle of restored energy. The Food Captains are the cornerstones to providing a first class lunch between the morning and afternoon heats, and a barbecue after the regatta. The food restores energy to the rowers, the parents, and coaches. Equally important, the feast creates a positive environment that adds enthusiasm and positive mental energy back into the entire team and its supporters. An uplifting karma for all associated with the crew is generated, and an overall victory is well underway, regardless of what happens on the water!

Winning the War

The battles of perception and restored energy are important, but the whole war is won by the parents of the team who make a harmonious contribution to the whole event. In these days of fan and parent rage in sports, the sport of crew comes with a higher calling. It is a flashback to the old college days when sports were good, old-fashioned fun and not just a business. We all could take a lesson from the English tradition found in rugby where the teams beat the snot out of each other on the field, but then rub elbows in a pub after the match. The parents who can extend friendly communication and sportsmanship to all the other teams, parents, and coaches win the crew war. Crewing is a cult inbred with a lot of people who "eat and sleep" the sport. Because it is small in numbers, but not in hearts, it is especially important to extend this feeling of camaraderie and friendliness. After all, every parent has a daughter at the race competing to her full abilities, and win or lose, nothing should be taken away from the total effort of each woman rower. This positive attitude creates a total parental victory and surpasses all other battles.

The total parent war was won when arch rival Notre Dame came to Michigan State on a Tuesday evening after a Saturday "wind out" (too windy to race). A barbecue was held after the race. When the parents of Michigan State invited the teams and parents of Notre Dame, there was a complete and pleasant surprise by the entire Notre Dame rowing community. Using the battle weapon of strawberry shortcake, this crew "crowd-pleaser" was an added attraction seldom seen by another team.

Who says, "To the victor belongs the spoils"? The battle and war of the parents is won by harmony to advance women's intercollegiate crew, a civilized sport.

CHAPTER 12

Crew Coverage

Many people attending a regatta, including the media, are clueless about the sport. I will agree that there are no digital scoreboards or giant video screens with which to understand the score, which race is running, or which team or individuals are in the boats. That is why, you, as a Crew Dad, must be your own photographer, statistician, and sometimes announcer.

My son played the guard position in high school football for Walsh Jesuit, a Greater-Cleveland area team. When the team visited Paul Brown Stadium in Massillon, Ohio, I knew I was in football heaven. After a 15-yard gain on the ground, the announcer said, "That play was made possible by the block from #64, Derrek Seif, the right guard." Normally an offensive guard only gets recognition when there is a holding penalty. In Massillon, not only do they know football, the media knows the subtleties of the game and gives credit to the whole team, even an offensive guard.

The same type of scenario was experienced with the announcer at Princeton when, before the start of the race, he would announce the names starting with the cox and then the rowers, stroke to bow. During the race, not only was the stroke's per minute given, but the team's effort and response to the other boats was clearly identified. I never forgot the words: "The Princeton team made a big deposit in the first 200 meters to take a boat length lead." The sweetest words by an announcer were at the Big Ten Championships in 2003 during my daughter's 2V8+ race when he said, "Michigan State is dominating this race."

Except for the NCAA Championship, many times the sound system is uneven and disrupted during the race, leaving much to the imagination of an anxious Crew Dad. After a few years of learning the sport and knowing what to do, we got imaginative and announced our own races.

After being at the regatta, I was never too impressed with most newspaper writers covering the events. If they covered the women's crew event, they were probably complete novice sportswriters themselves, so as to not get the assignment to cover fall football or spring baseball for the university. Therefore, the designated press who showed up, at least in the Midwest, usually didn't know an ergometer from an egg timer. Plus, if your daughter rows in the 1V8+, don't expect any pictures the next day in the newspaper. The media usually gets there early, takes a few pictures of the first race they see, and leaves, totally oblivious to the intense competition and more accomplished rowers who race later in the day. The coverage is normally better on the Coasts where a tradition and knowledge of the sport has developed.

There was one outstanding article about the Michigan State team written by Joe Rexrod of the *Lansing State Journal* on May 1, 2002. The article was full of pictures, and he praised the team and Coach Bebe Bryan's program for "growing in-state talent" into NCAA Championship-caliber rowers. At that time, the Spartans were ranked 12th in the nation. As a Crew Dad making a scrap book, don't expect front page articles in the local paper with giant action shots describing your daughter's team victory.

The best coverage for crew is through the internet. On the web, someone designated to cover the sport is writing about the team, spells out the times of the heats, and comments on both the quality and competitiveness of the event. Even though rowing is the ultimate team sport, I always enjoyed when they would put the names of each rower with the seat position so there was some recognition for the effort made at the regatta. All this information is on the sports site for the university, usually under the heading "W Crew" or "W Rowing."

In addition to each university website, my favorite information sources for knowing what's happening are:

www.USRowing.org   www.Row2K.com

These are the two rowing "cult" sites where people in-the-know go to find out the latest news about this great sport.

For major collegiate rowing regattas, a product and service company, Jamco™ (trademark of Kent Mitchell), has been serving the competitive rowing community since 1968. In addition to their race data collection and bulletins for high level competition, they operate real-time internet race results including 500-meter split times. Results include times and color graph positions of each team on the 500-meter splits. Without making a physical appearance, I was able to follow the 2004 NCAA Women's Championship *live* from Sacramento, California by dialing in www.jamcotimes.com/2004/ncaaw/index.htm.

There are also sites of conferences like www.bigten.org and sites of specific regattas like the Head of Ohio: www.threeriversrowing.org, where more detailed information can be obtained for a particular subject.

Although the local print media is usually pretty lame, there are a few bright spots in the national media coverage. *USA Today* does list the rankings every week for Division I Women when the spring season begins around the first part of April. The rankings are based on the performance of the 1V8+ boat with like opponents and head-to-head competition. Each week's rankings are listed on the internet, usually by midweek and are published in *USA Today* on the next to back page on Thursday or Friday.

The 50th Anniversary (November 10, 2003) issue of *Sports Illustrated* included 2,548 covers from 1954 to the November 2003 issue. Crew was on the cover twice. The Cornell men's crew team was pictured in the spring of 1962 and the Harvard men's crew team with famous coach, Harry Parker, was seen on the cover in June 1965. Coach Parker has guided the Harvard men's heavyweight team to national dominance and international acclaim over nearly four decades. It is tough to see this intensely competitive sport beat out in coverage by such "sports" as bridge card playing, dog and horse shows, chess and ballooning over the many issues of *Sports Illustrated*. In that same 50th anniversary issue, there was a section on sports in America that covered the great rowing tradition in Washington State, describing the Head of the Lake regatta, which signified host University of Washington's completion of their 101st year of rowing. It was disappointing to me that there was no mention of the Michigan State Women's Eight victory over fifteen outstanding teams, including well-recognized programs from University of Victoria, British Columbia, Virginia, Stanford, and hometown favorite, University of Washington. This three-mile victory is a big deal, but received zero recognition in the article.

After the NCAA Championships in spring of 2003, *Sports Illustrated* did a color picture and small write up of the Harvard-Radcliffe women who won the NCAA Regatta Championship at Eagle Creek Reservoir in Indianapolis. A later edition of the magazine honored Courtney Brown in "Faces in the Crowd." Ms. Brown was co-captain and 7th seat for the Harvard-Radcliffe team.

Although I am not so naïve as to think that women's crew should get top billing, it would be great to see a higher quantity of coverage and a better quality of articles for the amount of effort these young women put into the sport. I did see ESPN2 at both the Big Ten Championships, where Michigan State was interviewed, and at the NCAA Championships. Although we looked in the ESPN schedules for broadcasts, we never did see any TV coverage of these events.

The spirit of the sport and the pageantry of racing would make for a great documentary and chance to show the epitome of a team sport. The U.S. National Women's Team started practice on January 5, 2004, in Seattle, to compete in the 2004 Summer Olympic Games, August 14-22, 2004, in Athens, Greece. The Olympics has sweep rowing events in pairs and eight with coxswain, which will help create the recognition that women's rowing deserves.

12.1 ESPN Interview
Big Ten Championships 2003 - Columbus, Ohio

Although there are not a lot of books written about women's rowing or rowing in general, there are two good books that I enjoyed:

The Red Rose Crew by Daniel J. Boyne
Publisher: Hyperion, New York

The Book of Rowing by D. C. Churbuck
Publisher: The Overlook Press

Also, there is a lot of information contained in the regatta programs, the individual school publications, and a wealth of knowledge on the internet for the Novice Crew Dad to follow the sport and get fully engaged in all the happenings.

Besides my own photos and ones purchased off various internet sites, I printed all the information I could find to make a scrapbook each year, so as to record time spent in an often under-appreciated, but wonderful sport.

CHAPTER 13

"Rowed" to the Sweep 16

One of the most exciting sports events all year is the NCAA college basketball tournament labeled "March Madness." This single-elimination tournament, characterized by the "Initial 65," the "Sweet 16," the "Elite 8," and the "Road to the Final 4," truly identifies the national champion in the sport of basketball for both men and women. As a take-off of basketball, women's rowing could be labeled "May Madness." It is this month that the big regattas take place for conferences and regions finalizing the bids for the NCAA Championship regattas. Tongue in cheek, I have labeled the NCAA Division I finals as "Rowed to the Sweep 16." Making up this total of sixteen rowing programs, twelve teams are invited to bring both their varsity eights as well as first varsity four, while four additional teams are invited to only bring their first varsity eight.

The NCAA Championship is held at the end of the spring sprint season and is the culmination of women's collegiate crew. It is a three-day event, usually beginning the last Friday in May, with universities from all over the U.S. competing for a national championship. Women's collegiate rowing became an official varsity sport in 1997. The NCAA Women's Rowing Championships have been hosted by four different sites around the country in its young, eight-year history. Sacramento, California will repeat as the host site in 2005.

Year	Host University	NCAA Championship Location
1997	California State University (aka: Sacramento State)	Sacramento, California
1998	University of Central Florida Lake Lanier Rowing Club	Gainesville, Georgia
1999	California State University (aka: Sacramento State)	Sacramento, California
2000	Univ. of Pennsylvania/Eastern Collegiate Athletic Conference	Camden, New Jersey
2001	University of Central Florida Lake Lanier Rowing Club	Gainesville, Georgia
*2002	Indiana University U.S. Rowing	Indianapolis, Indiana
2003	Indiana University	Indianapolis, Indiana
2004	California State University (aka: Sacramento State)	Sacramento, California
2005	California State University (aka: Sacramento State)	Sacramento, California

* 2002 was first year of 3 separate division championships (I, II, III)

Although relatively little has been written about this event of highly conditioned women athletes, the NCAA Championship is the most prestigious event in women's collegiate crew. Its competitiveness has ramped up exponentially over a short seven-year history.

Now three divisions (I, II and III) compete in the NCAA Championships making it a colorful spectacle of twenty-two teams and six institutions with 1V8+ only boat entries. In Division I, twelve teams across the country are invited along with four at-large schools who race with their 1V8+ shell only. The 1V8+ is considered the highest level of competition and is the category where a school's national ranking originates during the regular spring season.

In Division II and III, there are four and six teams respectively who are invited to compete for their Divisional NCAA Championships. Starting in 2004 for Division II, two at-large schools brought just their 1V8+ shells, similar to Division I. Divisions II and III began competing for their NCAA Championships at the same time as Division I in

Indianapolis in 2002. With all three divisions at the finals, it illustrates the growing popularity and competitive level for women's crew.

Regional Alignment

The divisions in women's NCAA rowing are divided into geographic regions. Although there is some competition in the year across regions, most of the schools compete within their region because of travel distance to transport the shells and teams, as well as to establish conference and regional champions. As of 2004, there are 143 women's crew teams competing at the university level: 85 in Division I, 16 in Division II, and 42 in Division III.

In order to get a good understanding of the schools, the divisions, and the regions, I have listed them in matrix form. *(pages 122-123)*

Division I Schools / 5 Regions				
New England	*Mid-Atlantic*	*South*	*Central*	*West*
Boston College	Bucknell U	U of Central Florida	U of Cincinnati	California State U, Sacramento
Boston U	U at Buffalo, state U of New York	Clemson U	Creighton U	U of California, Berkeley
Brown U	Colgate U	Duke U	U of Dayton	U of California, Irvine
U of Connecticut	Columbia U-Barnard College	Jacksonville U	Drake Univ	U of California, Los Angeles
Dartmouth College	Cornell U	U of Louisville	Eastern Michigan U	Gonzaga U
Fairfield U	U of Delaware	U of Miami (FL)	Indiana U, Bloomington	Loyola Marymount U
Harvard U	Drexel U	U of North Carolina, Chapel Hill	U of Iowa	Oregon State U
College of the Holy Cross	Duquesne U	Southern Methodist U	U of Kansas	U of San Diego
U of New Hampshire	Fordham U	Stetson U	Kansas State U	San Diego State U
Northeastern U	George Mason U	U of Tennessee, Knoxville	U of Michigan	Santa Clara U
U of Rhode Island	George Washington U	U of Texas at Austin	Michigan State U	U of Southern California
Sacred Heart U	Georgetown U	University of Tulsa	U of Minnesota, Twin Cities	St. Mary's College of California
Yale U	Iona College	U of Virginia	Murray State U	Stanford U
	La Salle U		U of Notre Dame	U of Washington
	Lehigh University		Ohio State U	Washington State U
	Loyola College (Maryland)		U of Wisconsin, Madison	
	Marist College			
	U of Massachusetts Amherst			
	U of Pennsylvania			
	Princeton U			
	Robert Morris U			
	Rutgers, State U of NJ, New Brunswick			
	St. Joseph's U			
	Syracuse U			
	Temple U			
	U.S. Naval Academy			
	Villanova U			
	W. Virginia U			
13	28	13	16	15
Grand Total 85				

CHAPTER 13 ROAD TO THE SWEEP 16

| Division II Schools / 3 Regions |||
East	South	West
Assumption College	Barry U	*U of California, Davis
U of Charleston, West Va	Florida Institute of Technology	U of California, San Diego
Dowling College	Lynn University	Humboldt State U
Franklin Pierce College	Nova Southeastern University	Seattle Pacific U
Mercyhurst College	Rollins College	Western Washington U
	U of Tampa	
5	6	5
Grand Total 16		

* Univeristy of California, Davis will begin reclassification to Division I in fall 2004

| Division III Schools / 4 Regions ||||
New England	New York	Mid-Atlantic	Pacific
Bates College	Cazenovia College	Bryn Mawr College	Chapman University
Clark University (Massachusetts)	Hobart and William Smith Colleges	Johns Hopkins U	Lewis and Clark College
Colby College	Ithaca College	Marietta College	Mills College
Connecticut College	State U of New York Maritime College	Mary Washington College	Pacific Lutheran U
Hamilton College	Rochester Institute of Technology	North Park University	U of Puget Sound
Lesley U	Skidmore College	Richard Stockton College of New Jersey	Willamette University
Massachusetts Institute of Technology	St. Lawrence University	Trinity College (District of Columbia)	
Massachusetts Maritime Academy	U.S. Merchant Marine Academy	Washington College (Maryland)	
Mount Holyoke College	Union College (NY)		
Simmons College	Vassar College		
Smith College			
Trinity College (Connecticut)			
Tufts U			
U.S. Coast Guard Academy			
Wellesley College			
Wesleyan U (Connecticut)			
Williams College			
Worcester Polytechnic Institute			
18	10	8	6
Grand Total 42			

Selection for NCAA Championship

The teams are selected by the NCAA Women's Rowing committee for each division. The Division I rowing committee has seven members with at least one member from each of the five regions. This committee is both nominated and selected by the Division I governing structure and has a designated number of coaches and athletic directors. According to the 2002 NCAA Championship program, the selection criteria has the following common elements across Division I and II: "Selection of the teams are based on eligibility and availability of student-athletes, regional championship results, regional rankings, results against teams/boats already selected, results against regionally-ranked teams, head-to-head results, and late season performance." Division III has most of Division I and II selection criteria; however, Division III does not establish regional champions, but looks at winning percentages and results against common opponents in the selection process.

With these criteria, the representative NCAA selection committee for each division chooses the following number of teams and boats that make up each team:

Division	Teams / Boats	Boat Types
I	12	1V8+, 2V8+, 1V4+
	*4	1V8+
II	4	1V8+, 2V8+
	**2	1V8+
III	6	1V8+, 2V8+

*4   Universities are represented only with one V8+ boat
**2   At large 1V8+ - selected beginning in 2004

Divisions II and III

Beginning in 2002, qualifying schools from Division II and III were invited to the NCAA Championships to crown a champion for their respective divisions. In Division II, University of California at Davis earned a maximum of 50 points in 2002 to take the title. By repeating as Division II champs in 2003, they decided to reclassify to Division I in the fall of 2004. Mercyhurst captured the 2004 Division II NCAA Championship. Nova Southeastern's debut in 2004 was a first place in the V8+ Petite Final. This school had no rowing program prior to winning this event, and they did it with all novices. This is another indication of the rapid advancement of women's rowing.

The 2002 inaugural NCAA Division III Championship belonged to Williams College. Colby took the title in 2003, followed by Ithaca College in 2004.

The "Sweep 16" Division I

The Division I Championship is comprised of twelve teams where each team fields three boats, 1V8+, 2V8+, and 1V4+. In addition, there are four 1V8+ boats selected that do not participate in team competition but row in the main 1V8+ event, rounding out the "Sweep 16."

The make-up of the twelve teams is done by selecting one from each of the five regions (usually regional champion), with the remaining seven teams chosen at-large. The four universities that are selected for inclusion of their 1V8+ boats only are chosen at-large as well.

The seven-member committee makes the bids right after the regional championships (always by Tuesday after the Sunday regional finals). Just like in the NCAA March Madness Basketball Tournament, there are clear-cut bids, and a host of criteria is applied and voted on by the committee.

In 2003, the Michigan State team tied for the Big Ten Championships in points and had a 2V8+ Big 10 Championship boat. The 1V8+ finished third at the Big Ten, but less than a second behind 2nd place Ohio State. At the South/Central Regional Championships, the 2V8+ again took the gold medal, but the 1V8+ placed 6th at the regionals. At that time, we wondered if we would get an NCAA Championship bid. Given the strength of the entire team and the success of the 2V8+, the committee selected M.S.U. to compete in the NCAA Championships in Indianapolis.

Again in 2004, on the overall strength of the team's performance, M.S.U. received an NCAA Championship team bid. They were joined by Big Ten opponents: Michigan, Ohio State, and Wisconsin. Rounding out the twelve teams for the trip to Sacramento were: Brown, California (Berkeley), Harvard, Princeton, Virginia, Washington, Washington State, and Yale. Completing the 2004 "Sweep 16" with their first varsity eight-boats were: Notre Dame, Southern California, Tennessee, and Texas. Brown University won their fourth NCAA Division I Championship with firsts in both eight-boat events and a third in the V4+. Regardless of the outcome, a bid to the NCAA Championships is an enviable achievement for crew programs, whether in Division I, II, or III!

The NCAA Finals

I was fortunate to attend two NCAA Championships, both in Indianapolis, and both with my daughter competing in an event. The NCAA, U.S. Rowing, and University of Indiana were perfect hosts to both the 2002 and 2003 NCAA Championships. Eagle Creek Reservoir has a wonderful viewing area as the start can be viewed through binoculars, and the finish is immediately in front of the grandstands located next to the judges' tower. Except for the weather getting a little "iffy" at times with late May thunderstorms, the course is excellent for spectators, and is fair in all lanes for the teams competing.

13.1   Electronic welcome sign
NCAA Championships 2003
Indianapolis, Indiana

As you would expect, there is much more seriousness at this event as the "crème de la crème" compete for the National Championship. The normally relaxed faces of the women rowers draw tense, as game-faces are everywhere.

Being a championship, the regatta exudes the professionalism demanded for a national championship setting. The announcing and communication system is clear, the launch boats are trim and neat, and the judges are very exact in their proceedings. This is one time where the spirit of crew is not faceless. Rowers have names and are announced by seat before each race. Teams are identified and listed by their season accomplishments. The scoring is exact, timely, and posted for all to follow. In case you or your Scoring Captain want to keep your own tabulation, I have devised a scoring sheet to help you score the NCAA Championship for Division I. There are twelve teams and four at-large 1V8+ boats for which to score points. Perhaps this matrix could be added to the NCAA program to help all parents track the championship:

13.2 View from the finish line
Eagle Creek - NCAA Championships 2002-03
Indianapolis, Indiana

	NCAA Division I Scoring Sheet					
	Team Name	Place	1V8+ Points	2V8+ Points	1V4+ Points	Total Points
1						
2						
3						
4						
5						
6						
7						
8						
9						
10						
11						
12						

	*At-large 1V8+	Place	1V8+ Points	--	--	--
1						
2						
3						
4						

Points Awarded
Event/Place

	1	2	3	4	5	6	7	8	9	10	11	12
1V8+	36	33	30	27	24	21	18	15	12	9	6	3
2V8+	24	22	20	18	16	14	12	10	8	6	4	2
1V4+	12	11	10	9	8	7	6	5	4	3	2	1

*If any of these 1V8+ place in the top 12, their points are awarded to the next "team" boat.

Although slightly sad because it marks the end of the road for that year's rowing competition, in my opinion, it doesn't get any better than walking down the "Rowed to the Sweep 16" and experiencing the Division I, II, and III NCAA Championships.

CHAPTER 14

Big Ten Breaks the Ice

We were all huddled around our Scoring Captain, for it was the last and deciding race of the 2003 Big Ten Championships. Our Michigan State team had done extremely well throughout the day with all six shells qualifying for the Grand Finals. It was a total display of all-around team talent with all boats including the novice eights and fours scoring well. Our 2V8+, with my daughter sitting fifth seat, had just won the 2V8+ competition, which was the second Big Ten Championship boat in M.S.U. rowing history. The last race, 1V8+, would decide the team championship.

14.1 M.S.U. Gold Medal Victory Carry
2V8+ Big Ten Championships 2003
Columbus, Ohio

All of the parents were like little kids, jumping up and down and demanding from our Scoring Captain, Peter Thomas, what the situation was. To win the Big Ten Team Championship, we needed to finish first or second in the 1V8+, or Ohio State had to beat Michigan. Our 1V8+ boat made a great effort and finished with a strong sprint, but the University of Michigan won, followed by Ohio State, and

M.S.U. was third by seven-tenths of a second behind O.S.U. With that order of finish of the last race, it created a tie for first place in the overall team point total: Michigan State-123 and University of Michigan-123.

That's when the tie-breaker became a stark reality for us. The rules state that if there is a tie in points, first place goes to the team that wins the 1V8+ race. Duffy Daughterty, famous football coach at Michigan State, once said, "A tie is like kissing your sister." Even though, as parents, our feeling was worse than kissing your sister, the M.S.U. team had finished the best ever in the young Big Ten Championships. At the same regatta, Iowa finished their best ever in fourth place, and recorded their first in history Big Ten Championship boat with their second varsity four. Wisconsin continued their strong showing with first places in both novice eight-boats. With Minnesota and Indiana programs developing, the Big Ten rowing conference came of age in 2003.

The Coasts Set the Trends

As with most trends in the United States, they start on either coast and work themselves toward the middle. It has been no different for the history of women's rowing. Following the men's rich rowing tradition on the East Coast, the women of the Ivy League schools followed suit. The oldest modern-day women's program in the Ivy League was founded in 1971 at Radcliffe. The Harvard Department of Athletics took over the administration of Radcliffe athletes, creating the Harvard-Radcliffe women's team. They row under the black and white colors of Radcliffe and were the NCAA Champions in 2003.

Brown University, located in Providence, Rhode Island, is another East Coast school steeped in rowing tradition. The Brown Bears Women's Crew was established in 1974, and has claimed four Division I NCAA Championships out of the eight held, finishing in the nation's top five over the last ten years. There are many other schools in both the New England and Mid-Atlantic regions where rowing got an early beginning, resulting in quality women's programs.

The West Coast also has schools who developed women's programs early. At the University of Washington, a club team was formed in 1969. The program accelerated quickly as they became National Champions in 1970. University of Washington has won three of eight Division I NCAA Championships.

At the University of California, crew became the first sport at the time the university was founded in 1868. The women's crew program is 30 years old, as the sport began to flourish in 1974. Stanford's women's rowing started as a club in 1971 and received varsity status in 1986. The West Coast, with its mild climate, bountiful water, and historic boat builders, have rivaled the East with its early history and crew tradition.

The Big Ten Conference

The Big Ten Conference, founded in 1896, has a long tradition of competitiveness among men and women student-athletes. With the addition of Penn State University in 1990, the conference is known for an association of eleven top universities.

University	Joined Big Ten
University of Illinois	1896
University of Michigan	1896
University of Minnesota	1896
Northwestern University	1896
Purdue University	1896
University of Wisconsin	1896
University of Indiana	1899
University of Iowa	1899
Ohio State University	1912
Michigan State University	1949
Pennsylvania State University	1990

The schools, for the most part, are located in the Midwest. Geographically, it really was the Midwest in the 1850's when many of the schools were founded. Now, a better geography designation is really the central U.S., as Iowa is probably the only school now truly in the Midwest of the U.S.A.

To describe how things get out-of-date, the University of Michigan's famous fight song, "Hail to the Victors," chants Michigan as "Champions of the West." In 1896, it was the Western Conference, as the song alludes to.

The Big Ten schools have a great tradition in college football and other major sports that kids practice in the "snowbird country." Given the changing, often inclement, weather in this region, many of the women compete in indoor sports like volleyball, basketball, and swimming. With the four seasons, including four months of winter with iced-over lakes and rivers, rowing was something you did in a 12-foot wooden boat at the cottage from Memorial Day to Labor Day. Sweep rowing was certainly not in the hearts and minds of many people in Big Ten Country, and little was known about the sport until recently.

The year 2000 marked the inaugural season for the Big Ten Championships in women's crew. Six teams participated that year in Madison, Wisconsin, including crews from Indiana, Iowa, Michigan, Michigan State, Ohio State, and Wisconsin.

14.2 "Ice Team" rowing at Ann Arbor, Michigan Early spring 2003

It was a wonderful inaugural at picturesque Lake Wingra, an 1,850-meter course situated adjacent to the University of Wisconsin campus. The Big Ten's first championship was won by the University of Michigan, followed by Michigan State and Ohio State.

CHAPTER 14 BIG TEN BREAKS THE ICE

Of these six inaugural teams, the University of Wisconsin has the longest history. The Badgers are the anomaly to the early beginnings of women's crew on the East and West Coasts. This school has participated in women's open eights since 1895 and won "national titles" in 1975 and 1986 before the official NCAA Championships. Wisconsin has produced thirteen U.S. Olympic rowers since the 1976 Montreal Olympic debut. The other five inaugural schools began their programs around the time that rowing became an official NCAA sport; Minnesota added women's varsity crew in 2001:

14.3   Big Ten Championships
Madison, Wisconsin 2000

Iowa	1994
Michigan and Ohio State	1996
Michigan State	1997
Indiana	1999
University of Minnesota	2001

Seven of the eleven universities of the Big Ten now have flourishing women's crew programs, all with approximately sixty women to a team, competing with the best programs in the nation.

In three of the other four universities, there are club rowing teams for women: Purdue, Northwestern, and Penn State. Illinois is the only Big Ten school with no connection to rowing, however, they are not "a river runs through it" university. No water, no row. Penn State is the other school most challenged without water nearby. My daughter, Lindsay, actually introduced us to the sport as a club crew stroke in State College, Pennsylvania. The club had a setback when their practice lake at Stone Valley was drained, but in typical crew desire, the Penn State rowing club goes on.

The seven Big Ten conference schools with sanctioned varsity crew teams continue to enhance their programs. University of Michigan and Michigan State both built new boathouses with first class workout rooms, rigging, and storage facilities, all equipped with state-of-the-art shells and fitness aids to raise the level of competition.

At The Ohio State University, a new and improved boathouse was built next to the women's practice and home racing site at Griggs Reservoir. As mentioned previously, the University of Wisconsin has great facilities and is currently enhancing its boathouse located at the Madison Campus. Indiana, Iowa, and Minnesota are also investing in their programs for continuous improvement. Quality equipment, practice environment, and facilities are essential watermarks to advance rowing programs to NCAA Championship caliber.

14.4 Michigan State University Boathouse

14.5 Michigan State University Boathouse Dedication-2002

The culmination of the Big Ten season is the Big Ten Championships. Four other schools have hosted these championships since the 2000 inaugural event at the University of Wisconsin. In 2001, the University of Michigan held the championships in Belleville, Michigan just east of Ann Arbor. There, U. of M. repeated as Big Ten champions and were excellent hosts to the event. Positioned next to the new boathouse on the water, the viewing hill for the 2001 Big Ten Championships was spectacular.

Michigan State hosted the 2002 Big Ten's at Lake Ovid, just north of East Lansing. This is a new site located at a

CHAPTER 14 BIG TEN BREAKS THE ICE 135

14.6 University of Michigan Boathouse

state park with plenty of room and a great grassy hill to view the races. The last event of the 1V8+ was the most exciting race I had seen as a crew Dad.

Beautiful Upper Arlington, a suburb of Columbus, Ohio was the site of the 2003 Big Ten Championships, hosted by Ohio State at the gorgeous setting of Griggs Reservoir on the Scioto River. Here you have a chance to walk, ride a bike, or drive a car down the riverbank and view the start of the race, staked at the dock. The reservoir is a beautiful setting for the racers with a tree-lined course and beautiful homes along the way.

The 2004 Big Ten Championship was held at the University of Iowa. The university is located in Iowa City, Iowa, and the regatta took place at the team's home course located on nearby Lake McBride. It was the fifth site to host the championship in its five-year history, which began in 2000. All of the teams showed increased competitiveness with the championship being decided by the last race. For the second year in a row, the University of Michigan rallied to win the 1V8+ race and captured the Big Ten title. In its five-year history, the University of Michigan has won four times and The Ohio State University has won once.

The Big Ten Conference has developed strong programs in women's crew and has had great representation at both the South/Central and NCAA Championships. In 2004, four of the twelve teams to receive an NCAA Championship bid were represented by the Big Ten Conference. For schools with a young history, the Big Ten teams have "broken the ice" to become national contenders in women's intercollegiate rowing.

CHAPTER 15

Beyond Rowing

No Crying in Crew

Ask your daughter or anyone who has tried it - rowing is one of the most comprehensive conditioning sports that there is. The sport demands stamina, endurance, quickness, strength, technique, the ability to endure pain, and most of all, heart.

In a sprint, as you cross the 1,500-meter mark of a 2,000-meter race, the oxygen in the body has been depleted and replaced by lactic acid, the fluid that fuels pain to the body. In the last 500 meters, as the cox calls out a series of Power 10's into the drive to the finish, the ultimate test is created of how much the mind, body, and spirit can endure. The last stroke past the finish line with the sound of the horn reduces the entire body to a mere fold of itself, seen from the shore as a slump, and felt by the rower as total exhaustion. It has been said that rowing a 2,000-meter sprint is like a continuous set of leg presses, ending when you can't "go" anymore.

To be a competitive rower, it takes tremendous dedication in both practicing and conditioning. Athletes get up at the "ass crack" of dawn for practice sets on the water, go through grueling erg tests, overload their muscles on weight machines, and take care of the shell and rigging. This sport leaves no room for whining and complaining. In fact, there is a taste of military discipline in crew, created by the precision movements, drill sergeant-like commands, and attention to details. Crew members who miss practice, break rules, or don't go to class find themselves excused from the team. There is no catering to primadonnas or star athletes who think they are better than the rest. To paraphrase from the movie, *A League of Their Own*, "There's no crying in crew!"

Ultimate Team Sport

With requirements for exactness, crewing is the ultimate in teamwork. In no other sport are you so dependent on the mirror image of your teammates, for the slightest imprecision of timing, balance, or technique can have a huge effect on speed and forward motion. When you look at the synchronous motion of an 8+ crew team, you may wish for such perfection in your occupation. If everyone in the working world could be in harmony like the fluid motion of a crew team, a new level of excellence could be achieved.

Bebe Bryans, coach of Michigan State from 1997-2004, stated, "Rowing is a sport where the individual has the opportunity to be excellent. Along with individual excellence, crew demands the ability to blend, so that who you are and what you do creates a team that is more than the sum of all the rowers and their efforts." When you view a team sprinting in the last 250 meters who are in "swing," you realize that the whole becomes greater than the sum of its parts. In rowing, there is an investment of effort to make the action effortless. Although synergy and togetherness is talked about in the business world with corporate teams and cross-functional groups, you can actually witness it in a crew when eight rowers become one in a magical fluid motion.

Heart and Emotion

Emotion drives most sports. Emotion is created by heart, and it's the heart that makes great athletes and great rowers. The former great basketball coach of the Boston Celtics, Red Auerbach, said he would hire heart over talent any day.

Red, in his book *MBA, Management by Auerbach*, said: "Most of all, I want someone who's willing to pay the price, who's willing to work at winning, who wants to win so badly that the person will give me everything he or she's got."

Bebe Bryans described the perfect "10" female rower as 6'2," 180 lbs., long-limbed, and well-proportioned with a flexible, lower body, and large lung capacity. Besides physique, the best rower has to be tough as nails with a strong mental will. She also said she would take a woman 5'7," 150 lbs., with a big heart who could out-pull a taller, more skilled rower. Big hearts not only make successful rowers, but successful people.

Managing the emotional part of a crew team is as important as managing the physical aspects of the sport. Having coached both men's and women's basketball, I would unequivocally say that managing the emotions of a women's team is far more challenging and more critical to success. Stored negative energy can lead to a team's disruption. In a 2000-meter sprint, a rower takes her body to the physical limits. Undue stress between members can cause the whole team to snap, sucking life's energy from their performance. Managing positive and negative emotions is another part of life's lessons learned from rowing.

Return of the Student Athlete

There has been a lot of controversy about Title IX and whether this NCAA act offers the correct ratios for women's sports. Having two daughters, I am obviously in favor of the ruling for equality in sports. It is especially pleasing when programs like Michigan State attract and recruit local talent. This allows local female athletes to pursue their dreams the same as the male athletes. It was a thrill for me to see my daughter "walk on" the crew team, achieve varsity status as a freshman, and row three of her four years at the NCAA Championships. This was a real credit to the coaching ability of Bebe Bryans, Matt Weise, and the entire staff, exemplified by the program's success in its short seven-year history. In all seven years, Michigan State women's crew was represented at the NCAA Championship; five team bids, and two first varsity eight-boat bids.

Not only does the new chance for equality in athletics present opportunities for young women to display their athlete ability, it creates an out-of-the-classroom experience that prepares them for life. At Michigan State, like other universities, the entire student experience was fostered. Many of the women achieve a high academic stature supported and encouraged by the coaches. The discipline demanded of crew carries over to the discipline required for excellence in the classroom. There is no pampering or special dispensation for women who do not go to class or who do not pull passing grades. Although the importance of education is instilled by the rowing program, rowers succeed in the classroom because they have an innate sense of pride in what they do. The values learned on the erg and on the water translate directly to the paper, presentation, or project done for school. "No regrets" is the crew creed. Rowers strive to have pride in everything they accomplish. The reason why this value of pride and integrity is so ingrained in a rower is because it is mandatory for the sport. No erg test could be completed, no race could be finished, no weight training session could be accomplished without that rower's desire to reach perfection. The term student-athlete in rowing is by no means an oxymoron.

Special Father-Daughter Relationship

In a close knit family, there is always a special relationship between a father and daughter. This bonding gets even tighter when both have experienced sports, and is the best when both played the same sport. I never rowed, but with my sports history, I could closely identify with the training, the commitment, the effort, and the competitiveness that my daughters experienced. Rowing brings together great men-women relationships. It has enhanced the relationship between both my daughters and me and stimulated the closeness between my son and his two sisters. A father who has been active in sports knows the dedication required, which further binds the connection with his daughter who has put forth her mind, soul, and body to be a competitive athlete. The relationship is in the "name of the father and the daughter."

Sisterhood

Building on the idea that rowing promotes strong relations between individuals, like other female sports, a profound sense of respect is established between women rowers. In a world where the opportunities available to women are still not equal to those available to men, the strong relationships between grounded, well-rounded, and independent women is invaluable. Women collegiate rowers are exposed to phenomenal role models that do not settle for the expectations put on them by society. Beyond having female role models in coaches, staff, and past rowers, they find role models in each other. Female rowers get to the point to which they are no longer racing for themselves, but instead for the other rowers in the boats and on their teams. One of the most inspiring things a coxswain can say is another rower's name during a race. Sometimes she will call down the boat, directing the boat to pull for each individual, one at a time. Not only does this help to unite the boat, this respect and love promotes a type of sisterhood outside of the shell that lasts a lifetime. Women's rowing teaches females to build a community of support and compassion amongst each other; a rare phenomenon in today's professional world.

Life's Preparation - A Rower's Point of View

Over the course of four years, I had a lot of personal interaction with my daughter and her teammates about what crew taught them about life. Jill Drexler, a 2004 1V4+ NCAA Championship medalist for Michigan State, responded to the question, "How has crew changed your life?" She said, "On a light note, I am definitely more comfortable walking around in public in my un-makeup and un-showered self. But seriously, I believe that rowing is the hardest thing I have ever done in my life. I have never played a sport where I have pushed myself to the limit day after day. The best thing about rowing is that every day I get to row with friends that I will have forever." My daughter, Kirsten, responded to the same question, "In challenging sports like rowing, I am sure every athlete asks herself the question, 'Is the pain I go through day-in and day-out worth the effort?' My rowing career has taught me that if you go after something with everything you have, the results will take care of themselves. There is no doubt in my mind that rowing is worth the pain."

Preparing for a race is much like preparing for any of life's challenges. Both involve the need for a sound physical and mental state. To prepare for a race, the body must be nourished with the right kind and amount of food. For most people, seven hours of sleep is needed preparation. Stretching and taking deep breaths help the body achieve a relaxed state. This physical routine is the same as for any of life's endeavors.

I asked Krista Buzzell, an all-American stroke, about the mental preparation. Krista said, "Rowers prepare mentally by surrounding themselves with friends and family or meditating quietly, visualizing every 100 meters of a race that is about to happen. By clearing the mind of worried thoughts and doing a mental checklist of techniques and strategies, a calming effect is created for the upcoming task. Rowing teaches time management and the fact that if you work hard, you get to play hard. A positive mental attitude can completely change a really hard workout, just as it can change any of life's encounters. Rowing all-out for 2,000 meters takes persistence, but it's that persistence through the tough times that makes the best times that much sweeter. In crew, you learn that time goes fast. I learned that my four-year involvement with crew went by in a hurry."

As learned from these three quotes, the preparation and education from crew can be applied to achieve great results in any profession or in any of life's challenges. Rowing and life's preparations run together. Therefore, live and enjoy the moment at hand, "carpe diem," seize the day!

A Bright Future

When asked of Coach Bryans, "What should young women expect to gain from crew?" she replied, "Confidence, control of your own destiny, and becoming a fierce competitor. Crew creates lifelong friends surrounded by a positive approach."

As women's crew participation accelerates, we will hear about great women achievers in all walks of life who began their greatness with the virtues of rowing. Anita DeFrantz, a bronze medalist in the women's eight at Montreal in 1976, is an attorney who became the International Olympic Committee's first female vice president in 1997. Because the sport is in its infancy, it will be the current generation of women who will use their rowing background to create a better global society. Already women crew graduates are entering the fields of business, medicine, education, and other professional careers. Look for these women to excel in whatever they do with their foundation of character, strength, and confidence.

15.1 Co-author E. Zilly and K. Seif
Friends for Life

Rowing is not a win/lose sport. Sure there are Big Ten Champions, Regional Champions, and NCAA Champions. However, after four years as a Novice Crew Dad, I came to realize that anyone rowing at the collegiate level is a champion for life. The four "D's": Development, Determination, Discipline, and Dedication, all surrounded by the positive mental attitude of women's crew, stroke to bow, creates a Ph.D. in life's learning.

The glory for the Novice Crew Dad is the pure joy of watching your daughter grow and compete. The glory for your daughter is the thrill of competition, learning life's les-

15.2 Author Richard Seif and daughter, Kirsten

sons through sports, and the fellowship and camaraderie of fellow rowers that go beyond rowing.

I've been proud to be a Crew Dad and hope that your rowing journey will be, is, or has been as rewarding for you as it has been for my daughters and me.

THE LAST WORD

Even though this book's main author was the Novice Crew Dad, it is only fitting as a Crew Mom that I have the last word. Behind every good man and rowing daughter is a Crew Mom to help them get their sea legs. Just like in crew, our family has been a team, all rowing in the same direction. There are no leaky boats on the sea of family unity.

As a Crew Mom, I would like to thank all the coaches and staff who propel this great women's sport! My best goes to all the women who row and all the moms and dads who support their daughters. We all can learn from the lessons of crew to make the world a better place!

Carol Seif
Michigan State University - Crew Mom

SOURCES

BOOKS
Auerbach, Red, M.B.A. *Management by Auerbach*. Macmillan Publishing Company, 1991.
Boyne, Daniel J. *The Red Rose Crew*. Hyperion, 2000.
Churbock, D.C. *The Book of Rowing*. The Overlook Press, 1999.
Wallace, Carol McD. *The Greatest Baby Name Book Ever*. Avon Books-New York 1998.
Poynter, Dan. *Writing Nonfiction*. Para Publishing, 2000.

PERIODICALS
Carton, Barbara. "Colleges Have Plenty of Money for Tall, Muscular Women; No Experience Necessary," *Wall Street Journal*, May 14, 1999.
Macur, Juliet. "Rowing Scholarships Available, No Experience Necessary,"*New York Times*, May 28, 2004
McDonell, Terry. "The Cover Story," *Sports Illustrated Magazine*, November 10, 2003.
Wahl, Grant. "Water World," *Sports Illustrated Magazine*, November 17, 2003.

NCAA EVENT PROGRAMS
Big Ten Conference Championships. University of Wisconsin, University of Michigan, Michigan State University, The Ohio State University, 2000, 2001, 2002, 2003.
Head of the Ohio. Three Rivers Rowing Association, Mercy Foundation, 2000, 2002.
Head of the Schuykill Regatta. University Barge Club of Philadelphia, 2000.
Lexus Central Sprint. University of Tennessee, 2000, 2003.
Media Guide. Michigan State Women's Crew, Michigan State University, 1999, 2000.
Princeton Open Crew. Princeton University, 2002.
NCAA Championships. University of Pennsylvania, ECAC, 2000.
University of Indiana. US Rowing, 2002, 2003.

MOVIES
Ben-Hur. Directed by William Wyler, MGM, 1959.

INTERNET SITES
Aidans.boat_club/erg_info.php; www.rowinghistory.net; www.vespoli.com; www.Friendsofrowing.htm; www.USRowing.org; www.Row2Kcom; www.BigTen.org; www.NCAA.org; www.Pocock.com; www.MSU.edu; www.MSU.crew.com; www.tricklefan.com; wosport@aol.com; www.jamcotimes.com

ARTICLES
Spartan Women's Crew Technique 206, Fall 2002.

PICTURE ACKNOWLEDGEMENTS

0.1	L to R	M. Weise, B. Bryans
0.2	L to R	E. Robertson, A. Johnson, J. Pickler, K. Seif, R. Seif, T. Middleton, H. Underwood
1.1	F to B	2002 1V8+ Ohio State, 1V8+ Michigan, 1V8+ Michigan State
1.2	L to R	K. Buzzell, K. Seif, S. Hicks
2.1	L to R	H. Wallerick, M. Myers (hidden), L. Seif, K. Fordney (hidden), E. Burns
4.1	Cox to Bow	E. Ferry, A. Pennington, K. Seif, H. Underwood, E. Robertson, J. Pickler, K. Dooley, T. Middleton, A. Johnson

W CREW - STROKE TO BOW

4.2	Cox to Bow	E. Ferry, A. Pennington, K. Seif, H. Underwood, E. Robertson, J. Pickler, K. Dooley, T. Middleton, A. Johnson
4.3	Cox to Stroke	J. Springrose, H. Bishop, J. Drexler, T. Bowman, S. Atkinson
4.4	L to R	K. Gay, C. Brown, K. Seif, A. Silder, K. Isaacs
5.1		L. Seif
6.1	L to R	J. Boswell, K. Gay
6.2	Back Row	KellyYauk, J. Boswell, T. Middleton, K. Gay, Kate Yauk, K. Seif, A. Cleland
	Front Row	J. Drexler, C. Weddel
7.2	L to R	A. Pennington, K. Seif
10.1	Cox to Bow	M. Fix, K. Gay, L. Thomas, S. Hicks, C. Brown, R. Miller, K. Seif, A. Silder, K. Isaccs
10.2		B. Bryans
10.4	Cox to Bow	E. Ferry, A. Pennington, K. Seif, H. Underwood, E. Robertson, J. Pickler, K. Dooley, T. Middleton, A. Johnson
10.6	Cox to Bow	E. Ferry, A. Pennington, K. Seif, H. Underwood, E. Robertson, J. Pickler, K. Dooley, T. Middleton, A. Johnson
10.7	Center	B. Bryans
11.1	L to R	D. Miller, K. Underwood
11.2		2003 Michigan State Team
11.3	L to R	A. Johnson, T. Middleton, K. Dooley, J. Pickler, K. Seif, H. Underwood, E. Robertson, A. Pennington, S. Beiniks
12.1	L to R	Kelly Yauk, R. Miller, K. Seif, H. Underwood, T. Middleton
14.1	Cox to Bow	S. Beiniks, A. Pennington, E. Robertson, H. Underwood, K. Seif, J. Pickler, K. Dooley, T. Middleton, A. Johnson
14.2	Cox to Bow	S. Beiniks, A. Pennington, K. Seif, H. Underwood, E. Robertson, J. Pickler, K. Dooley, T. Middleton, A. Johnson
15.1	L to R	E.Zilly, K. Seif
15.2	L to R	R. Seif, K. Seif

WOMEN'S COLLEGIATE ROWING PROGRAMS
2004 HEAD COACHES

Division I – New England	
Boston College	Steve Fiske
Boston U.	Holly Hatton
Brown U.	John Murphy
U. of Connecticut	Jennifer Sanford
Dartmouth College	Molly McHugh
Fairfield U.	Andre Albert
Harvard U.	Liz O'Leary
College of the Holy Cross	Patrick Diggins
U. of New Hampshire	Sue Taylor
Northeastern U.	Joe Wilhelm
U. of Rhode Island	Julia Chilicki
Sacred Heart U.	John Turner
Yale U.	Will Porter

Division I – Mid-Atlantic	
Bucknell U.	Stephen Kish
U. at Buffalo	Rudy Wieler
Colgate U.	Jana Heere
Columbia U.	Mike Zimmer
Cornell U.	Melanie Onufrieff
U. of Delaware	Laura Slice
Drexel U.	Louis Renzulli
Duquesne U.	Katie Kirsten
Fordham U.	Ted Bonanno
George Mason U.	Paul Rassam
George Washington U.	Helen Betancourt
Georgetown U.	Jimmy King
Iona College	Kevin Murphy
LaSalle U.	Matt Bergin
Lehigh University	Paul Savell
Loyola College	Al Ramirez
Marist College	David Buckner
U. of Massachusetts	Jim Dietz
U. of Pennsylvania	Barb Kirch
Princeton U.	Lori Dauphiny
Robert Morris U.	Liz Jones
Rutgers	Max Borghard
St. Joseph's U.	Gerry Quinlan
Syracuse U.	Kris Sanford
Temple U.	Christine Deatrick
U.S. Naval Academy	Mike Hughes
Villanova U.	Jack St. Clair
W. Virginia U.	Nancy LaRocque

Division I – South	
U. of Central Florida	Leeanne Crain
Clemson U.	Susie Lueck
Duke U.	Robyn Horner
Jacksonville U.	Jim Mitchell
U. of Louisville	Richard Ruggieri
U. of Miami	Debra Morgan
U. of North Carolina	Sarah Haney
Southern Methodist U.	Doug Wright
Stetson U.	Charles Huthmaker
U. of Tennessee	Lisa Glenn
U. of Texas	Carie Graves
U. of Tulsa	Kevin Harris
U. of Virginia	Kevin Sauer

Division I – Central	
U. of Cincinnati	Tim Royalty
Creighton U.	Daniel Chipps
U. of Dayton	Geoff Dillard
Drake U.	Charlie DiSilvestro
Eastern Michigan U.	Pamela Besteman
Indiana U.	Steve Peterson
U. of Iowa	Mandi Kowal
U. of Kansas	Rob Catloth
Kansas State U.	Patrick Sweeney
U. of Michigan	Mark Rothstein
Michigan State U.	Matt Weise
U. of Minnesota	Wendy Davis
Murray State U.	Bill McLean
U. of Notre Dame	Martin Stone
Ohio State U.	Andy Teitelbaum
U. of Wisconsin	Bebe Bryans

Division I – West	
California State U.	Mike Connors
U. of California, Berkeley	Dave O'Neill
U. of California, Irvine	Carrie Chamberlain-Parsons
U. of California, L.A.	Amy Fuller
Gonzaga U.	Glenn Putyrae
Loyola Marymount	Patrick Kelly
Oregon State U.	Charlie Owen
U. of San Diego	Doug Thiemann
San Diego State	Jennifer Zebroski
Santa Clara U.	Stephanie Shepherd
U. of Southern California	Kelly Babraj
St. Mary's College, CA	Pasha Spencer
Stanford U.	Aimee Baker
U. of Washington	Eleanor McElvaine
Washington State U.	Jane LaRiviere

APPENDIX 151

Division II – East	
Assumption College	Mike O'Coin
U. of Charleston	Kevin Gruber
Dowling College	Boban Rankovic
Franklin Pierce College	Jefferson Allen
Mercyhurst College	Adrian Spracklen

Division II – South	
Barry U.	Paul Mokha
Florida Institute of Tech	Casey Baker
Lynn U.	Susan Saint Sing
Nova Southeastern U.	John Gartin
Rollins College	Shawn Pistor
U. of Tampa	Bill Dunlap

Division II – West	
*U. of California, Davis	Emily Plesser
U. of California, San Diego	Pattie Pinkerton
Humboldt State U	Robin Miggs
Seattle Pacific U.	Keith Jefferson
Western Washington U.	John Fuchs

* Moves to Division I – fall of 2004

Division III – New England	
Bates College	Andrew Carter
Clark U. (Massachusetts)	Erick Thiemke
Colby College	Stew Stokes
Connecticut College	Eva Kovach
Hamilton College	Mike Gilbert
Lesley U.	Dale Wickenheiser
Massachusetts Institute of Tech.	Susan Lindholm
Massachusetts Maritime Academy	Fran McDonald
Mount Holyoke College	Jeanne Friedman
Simmons College	Nikolay Kurmakov
Smith College	Karen Klinger
Trinity College (Connecticut)	Lyllah Martin
Tufts U.	Gary Caldwell
U.S. Coast Guard Academy	Steve Hargis
Wellesley College	Joan O'Hara
Wesleyan U.	Beth Emery
Williams College	Justin Moore
Worcester Polytechnic Institute	Jason Steele

Division III – New York

Cazenovia College	Brian Burns
Hobart & William Smith Colleges	Sandra Chu
Ithaca College	Becky Metz Robinson
State U. of New York Maritime College	Captain Rick Smith
Rochester Institute of Technology	Jim Bodenstedt
Skidmore College	Jim Tucci
St. Lawrence U.	Nick Huges
U.S. Merchant Marine Academy	Larry Muri
Union College (NY)	Tom White
Vassar College	Michael Alton

Division III – Mid-Atlantic

Bryn Mawr College	Carol Bower
Johns Hopkins U.	Stephanie Thompson
Marietta College	Karen Glowacki
Mary Washington College	David Shuster
North Park U.	Tim Grant
Richard Stockton College of New Jersey	Bob Kerstetter
Trinity College (District of Columbia)	Sara Stevenson
Washington College (Maryland)	Dr. Mike Davenport

Division III – Pacific

Chapman U.	Paul Wilkins
Lewis & Clark College	Tessa Spillane
Mills College	Wendy Franklin
Pacific Lutheran U.	Meredith Graham Lawyer
U. of Puget Sound	Sam Taylor
Willamette U.	Rod Mott

INDEX

A
A League of Their Own 138
Albano buoy 75
aligner 22,74
Auerbach, Red 138

B
Babcock, J. C. 63
Ben Hur 7,12
Berra, Yogi 110
bi-sweptual 24,40
blade 5,16,20,63,64,65,73,96,199
blisters 5,54,56
The Book of Rowing 117,147
boot 94
bow 16,19,29,31,35,36,76,93
bow ball 19,62
Bow Pair 28,29,30,31,54
Boyne, Daniel J. 38,117
Bryans, Bebe i,iii,vi,vii,3,91,138,139
bucket rig 22
button 20,64,65,76

C
C Finals 22
catch 6,23,29,35,42,45,49,63
check it down 24
Concept 2 41,43
Coxswain Seat 62
coxswain 18,25,85,92
cox box 20
crewmors 24,37

D
Dad Vail Rowing Championship v
Daughterty, Duffy 130
Le Baron Pierre de Coubertin 9
deck 1,19,35,62
DeFrantz, Anita 143
Dirigo 66
Divisions (I, II and III) 120
Dreissigacker brothers 43
drive 11,23,26,35,93,98,108,135,137

E
electrolytes 57
The Engine 1,30,31,33,34,28,36,46
erg queen 24,32,46
ergometer (erg) 21,42,43,114
ESPN2 116,117

F
feathering 23,38,56,64
FISA 8,91
flying 60,78,86,109
foot-stretchers 5,20,43,57,63

G
Grand Finals vi,22,79,129
gunnel 20,38,62

H
hatchet 65
head 22
Head of the Charles 85
Head of the Lake 71,84,90,116
Head of the Ohio 72,81,83
Head of the Schuylkill 84
"head" race 16,17,81,85,86,100
Henley Royal Regatta 8

I
Indoor Tank 48,49

J
Jamco™ 115

K
kinesthetic 39

L
lactic acid 1,24,47,48,50,55,57
Lake Washington Rowing Club 84,85
Lansing State Journal 114
launch 71,77,83,88,92,93,96,99,100,127
lightweight 5,68
Lombardi, Vince 55
loom 65

M
"Macon" blade 65

N
NASCAR 61,67,68,69,82,83,107
New York Times 10,12
novice *(definition)* 18

O
oar 20,65
oarlock 20,54,64,65
Olympic 4,9,17,73,88,91,94,117,133,143
open water 22,33,42,54

P
PR 24
Parker, Harry 116
Paterno, Joe 106
Petite Finals vi,22
Philadelphia Girls Rowing Club 8
piece 21,50,55,107
pitch meter 66
Pococks 8
pogies 54,65,98

port 4,23,26,28,37,38,62
Power 10 11,23,44,137
Princeton Open Crew 100

R
rating 21,26,44,45,55,73,74
recovery 6,23,35
The Red Rose Crew 38,117
regatta *(definition)* 22
repecharge "rep" 9,22
Resolute 66
rigger 20,62,63,64,65
run 11,23,27,29,32,78,90,101,142
rush the slide 24,63

S
sculling 22,81
2 Seat 30,34
3 Seat 30,34,54
4 Seat 30,34
5 Seat 331,.34,54
6 Seat 31,34
7 Seat 32,34,54
seat racing 21,25,26,55,56,58,59,89
Sedgeley Club 8
settle 23
shell 19
slide 23,29,43,45,63
slump 24,96,137
Smith, John L. 106
South/Central Championships 79,101,103,108
Speed Coach™ 20,66,97
split 21,28,41,43,44,45,46,115
Sports Illustrated 115,116,147
sprint race 33,72,94
sprints 22
squaring 16,23
stake 22,74,93,94,107
starboard 23,26,33,37,38
starter 23,74,94
stern 1,16,19,26,28,31,34,35,36,62,93
Stern Pair 28,31,35,36
Stroke 20
stroke rate 7,22,33,43
Sweep v,65,81,117,125,126,128,132
sweep rowing 22,81,117,132
swing 23,138

T
tank 21,48,49,53
taper 21,58
tapering 58,59
Team Chemistry 37
Three Rivers Rowing Club 83
Title IX vi,2,9,10,11,12,139
track bite 24

U
U.S. National Women's Rowing Association 8

University Barge Club of Philadelphia 84
U.S. Rowing rules 71

V
V4+ 19,34,36,46,77
V8+ 19,28,29,30,34,37,346,77,124,125
varsity *(definition)* 19
Vespoli 66
VO2 max 48

W
Waddell, Rob 46
Wall Street Journal 2,3,12,147
Way-Nugh 24
Weise, Matt i,vi,vii,75, 139
Windermere Collegiate Crew Classic 100
"wings" 20,64
World Indoor Rowing Championship 46
www.jamcotimes.com 115
www.Row2K.com 115
www.USRowing.org 115

ABOUT THE AUTHORS

Richard Seif is a graduate of Michigan State University with both a BS degree in engineering and an MBA in marketing. He works as a sales and marketing professional in Cleveland, Ohio. Mr. Seif served as both a coach and spectator for his three children for over 20 years in many sports endeavors. He became a rowing enthusiast when both his daughters adopted women's crew at the NCAA Division I level. Mr. Seif currently resides in Chagrin Falls, Ohio.

Ellen Zilly is a recent graduate of The Ohio State University and presently works for a marketing services agency in Chicago, Illinois. Ms. Zilly began her rowing career in 1997 as an Ohio State novice and competed predominately in the varsity four from 1998-2001. She served as co-captain in her senior year and received the Golden Buckeye Coach's Award for her exemplary performance. Ms. Zilly currently lives in Evanston, Illinois.

QUICK ORDER FORM

☐ Yes, please send me additional copies of *W Crew – Stroke to Bow*

    1 – 4 copies @ $14.95 each

    5 + copies @ $12.95 each

Quantity	Price	TOTAL U.S. $

Shipping & Handling Charges		
Order Amount Shipping Charge in Continental U.S.A. $ 1.00 to $ 65.00 $ 5.00 $ 65.01 to $135.00 $ 8.00 $135.01 to $270.00 $10.00 $270.01 and over 5%	Subtotal	$
	Ohio Sales Tax 7.25%	$
	Shipping & Handling	$
	TOTAL (U.S. Dollars only)	$

SOLD TO:
Name _____
Company _____
Address _____
City _____
State _____ Zip _____
Phone (_____) _____

SHIP TO:
Name _____
Company _____
Address _____
City _____
State _____ Zip _____
Phone (_____) _____

TO ORDER:
Fax Order # <u>440-951-2110</u>   Telephone Order <u>1-800-433-9544</u>

Order by Mail   <u>7181 Industrial Park Blvd. Mentor, OH 44060</u>   E-mail Order <u>KLangford@activitiespress.com</u>

INDICATE METHOD OF PAYMENT
☐ Check in the amount of $ _____
   (*Payable to Activities Press, Inc.*)

  ☐ VISA   ☐ MasterCard

Credit Card # _____

Exp. Date _____

Signature _____

Purchase Order #, if applicable
_____

Send check and order to:
   Activities Press, Inc., 7181 Industrial Park Blvd., Mentor, Ohio 44060 U.S.A.

Activities Press, Inc.

7181 Industrial Park Blvd. • Mentor, OH 44060
440-953-1200 • www.activitiespress.com

Commercial Printer Offering:
- ❖ One through six color offset printing
- ❖ In-house electronic prepress department
- ❖ Quality service and good value

Official Printer of the Lake County Captains, Class A Baseball Team